W9-CPH-144

SAVING YOUR
MARRIAGE
BEFORE IT STARTS

Devotional

RESOURCES BY LES AND LESLIE PARROTT

3 Seconds (by Les)
The Complete Guide to Marriage Mentoring
(and workbooks and video)
The Control Freak (by Les)
Crazy Good Sex (by Les)
Dot.com Dating
The First Drop of Rain (by Leslie)
Getting Ready for the Wedding
God Made You Nose to Toes (children's book by Leslie)
The Good Fight
Helping Your Struggling Teenager (by Les)
High-Maintenance Relationships (by Les)
The Hour That Matters Most
I Love You More (and workbooks and video)
L.O.V.E.
The Love List
Love Talk (and workbooks and video)
Love Talk Devotional
Making Happy
Meditations on Proverbs for Couples
The Parent You Want to Be
Questions Couples Ask
Real Relationships (and workbook and video)
Saving Your Marriage Before It Starts (and workbooks and video)
Saving Your Second Marriage Before It Starts
(and workbooks and video)
Seven Secrets of a Healthy Dating Relationship (by Les)
Soul Friends (by Leslie)
Trading Places (and workbooks)
You Matter More Than You Think (by Leslie)
You're Stronger Than You Think (by Les)
Your Time-Starved Marriage (and workbooks and video)

SAVING YOUR MARRIAGE BEFORE IT STARTS

Devotional

52 Meditations for Spiritual Intimacy

NEWLY EXPANDED EDITION OF *BECOMING SOUL MATES*

Drs. Les & Leslie Parrott

ZONDERVAN

Saving Your Marriage Before It Starts Devotional
Copyright © 1997, 2017 by Les and Leslie Parrott

Previously published as *Becoming Soul Mates*

Requests for information should be addressed to:
Zondervan, *3900 Sparks Dr. SE, Grand Rapids, Michigan 49546*

ISBN 978-0-310-34482-7 (hardcover)

ISBN 978-0-310-34483-4 (ebook)

Published in association with Yates & Yates, www.yates2.com.

Cover design: Ranjy Thomas / Flying Rhino
Cover photography: © Daniel Davis / Lightstock®
Interior design: Kait Lamphere

First Printing December 2016 / Printed in the United States of America

To Ron and Katie Robertson,
a couple whose love of each other
has weathered an unspeakable storm
because your marriage is anchored in the love of Jesus.

CONTENTS

WHY DAILY DEVOTIONS FOR COUPLES OFTEN FAIL

"It's my turn to read first!" Leslie hollered from the shower.

"No way! You read first last night," I shouted back.

"Pleeeease. Let me read the Old Testament passage first," said Leslie.

For about a week and a half—or up to the eighth chapter of Genesis, whichever came first—this exchange became routine for us. Each night we sparred with each other over who would read the Bible first during our devotional time. We had set our sights on reading the Bible clear through as a couple, and each night before we went to sleep we would take turns reading a passage from the Old Testament and then one from the New.

But after a few evenings, the focus of our lofty spiritual quest was more about sleep than Scripture. We fought over who got to read first, not because of our spiritual passion, but because that person could doze or even fall asleep while the other was reading his or her passage!

Spending a systematic, meaningful quiet time with each other, reading God's Word and praying, has never come easy for us. We have tried setting aside time in the morning. And we have tried it in the evening. Time of day seems to make little difference.

11

We could never stick to it and our times were never what we hoped for. Worst of all, the problem made us feel guilty. If we were good Christians, with God at the center of our marriage, wouldn't setting aside time to cultivate spiritual intimacy be something that would come easy?

Not hardly.

We know and admire couples who open their Bibles together after breakfast, read a passage, share their secrets, and kneel to pray. But that never seemed to be our style. We wake up at different times on different days. We don't have the same routine every day. And, to be honest, we need an activity that doesn't seem like a duty that hangs over our heads.

Still, we have a restless aching, each of us, not just to know God individually, but to experience God as a couple. But how? How do we really allow God to fill the soul of our marriage?

OUR SPIRITUAL QUEST

When researchers examined the characteristics of fulfilled couples who had been married for more than two decades, one of the most important qualities they found was "faith in God and spiritual commitment." We never needed scientists to tell us that spiritual meaning was important to our marriage. We knew it from the start. Marriage is not a superficial bonding, a mere machine that needs routine maintenance to keep it functioning. Marriage for us is founded upon a mutual exchange of holy pledges. It is ultimately a deep, mysterious, and unfathomable spiritual endeavor.

Some years ago we started a program for engaged and newly married couples that eventually became a book, his/her workbooks, and video kit called *Saving Your Marriage Before It Starts*—SYMBIS for short. More than a million couples have gone through this program, and for a number of years now we have formally and informally surveyed and interviewed many of them. In addition, we have interviewed many churchgoing couples who have been married for years. We wanted to learn how successful couples tend the soul of their marriage.

So we asked Christian couples to measure just how important spiritual intimacy in marriage is to them, often on a ten-point scale. And the answer was almost always the same: very important. Nearly every couple said they place a high value on spiritual intimacy.

But when we asked these same couples how satisfied they were with the current level of spiritual intimacy in their marriage, their answers again became predictable: not very satisfied. "We agree on tithing and stuff," one woman confided, "but we don't have any deep or meaningful conversations about spiritual matters." A husband told us, "I feel so uncomfortable praying with my wife. I mean she sees me seven days a week, she knows how I live!" So, for some time now, we have been on a quest to find a means to spiritual intimacy in marriage that works—for us and the couples in our program. This book is the result. We believe it provides the tools for you and your partner to have a consistent and meaningful time together that is both enjoyable and spiritually enriching.

USING THIS BOOK FOR ALL ITS WORTH

The key to making the *Saving Your Marriage Before It Starts Devotional* work for you is its flexibility. There is no one right way of using it. Think of this book as a resource you mold and fit to your personal style.

Since we found that a weekly approach works best for many couples, the book provides fifty-two sessions. You may have your own personal quiet time each day, but meeting once a week as a couple is critical to becoming soul mates—a couple that is mutually committed to spiritual growth. Once you establish a pattern (each Sunday evening, for example), you will find that these sessions become a spiritual refueling station for the soul of your marriage.

Here's how each session is organized:

OPENING THOUGHT

Each session begins with a brief devotional thought on a marriage-relevant topic. These openings contain references to Scripture that can be studied more in depth if you desire. You may also want to use these references for your individual study throughout the week. You may wish to read the opening devotional thought separately on your own, but we believe most couples will benefit from reading the passage aloud together.

FROM GOD'S WORD

The opening thought is followed by a passage of Scripture from the New International Version of the Bible that relates to the same topic. It is printed in the book to allow easy accessibility, but you may also want to read it in your own Bible to compare translations or to provide a fuller context. Either way, one of you can read the passage aloud.

YOUR TURN

Material for a brief time of discussion follows the Scripture reading. Several questions and suggestions encourage you to share relevant examples from your own lives. These questions and discussion starters are not meant to be completed in a hurry. The point is not to have your quiet time "checked off" your to-do list. If you are short on time, just select one or two of the questions. Don't feel that you need to answer every one every time.

SOUL TO SOUL

We have found that busy couples who are motivated to deepen their spiritual intimacy throughout a hectic week need to intentionally address three things: (1) what they gained as a couple from their session together; (2) what their partner is facing in the coming week that they will remember in their personal prayers; and (3) what they can do in a concrete way that will communicate kindness toward their partner in the coming week.

By addressing these three concerns *each week*, you strengthen and deepen your soul-to-soul connection. You will build a loving marriage bond of mutual appreciation and respect that is irreversible.

We call this part of your session "soul to soul," and it is at the heart of your quiet time together. To ensure that you are understanding your partner's soul and that you will remember their concerns in prayer, and that you will make a conscious plan for meeting their needs in the upcoming week, we recommend that you take notes. *Write down what you gained from your time together, what your partner's need is, and what you will do to increase the odds of them having a better upcoming week.*

PRAYER

Concluding each session is a printed prayer. Prayer is vital to healthy marriages but sometimes tough for married couples to do together. So we offer a simple prayer at the end of each session for you to read aloud or quietly by yourselves. We hope that these brief prayers will be a catalyst for the prayers of your heart.

REAL-LIFE SOUL MATES

Each session also contains material contributed by devoted couples who have found their own way of cultivating spiritual intimacy: real-life soul mates, if you will. In most but not all cases their words will reflect if only tangentially the main theme of the session. But the main point of these stories is to offer an inspirational glimpse into some of the most spiritually astute couples we know—of varying ages and seasons of married life. You will soon discover that every couple travels a unique route toward spiritual oneness. These real-life examples will help you and your partner chart your own course toward becoming soul mates.

OTHER WAYS OF BENEFITING FROM THE *SAVING YOUR MARRIAGE BEFORE IT STARTS DEVOTIONAL*

The most obvious way of using the *Saving Your Marriage Before It Starts Devotional* is to proceed from the first session to the last, week by week. But this is not necessary. You may choose to peruse the table of contents and turn selectively to the theme that seems relevant to you for that specific week. Feel free to choose session themes in the order that addresses your needs.

You might also consider using the *Saving Your Marriage Before It Starts Devotional* with a small group or in a Sunday school class for couples. For example, someone in the group could read aloud the Scripture passage and the opening thought. The group may even want to provide time for one-on-one discussion for couples and then reconvene for a lesson, an activity, or a group discussion.

One more thought. If you have not taken the SYMBIS Assessment, you may want to consider it. It takes just thirty minutes to complete online (each of you answers questions separately) and provides a powerful and personalized fifteen-page report. You'll discover your unique strengths as a couple and how your two personalities mesh. And in relationship to this book, it has a section devoted to helping each of you better understand the other when it comes to how you each feel closest to God and how you approach your spiritual lives. You can learn more (and find a certified SYMBIS facilitator in your area) at SYMBISassessment.com.

Your marriage relationship will either develop a depth that binds your two souls together, or it will experience a superficial bonding which rides the waves of emotion until the relationship is beached for lack of depth. So we offer a prayer for you. The yearning you and your partner have to be connected soul to soul can only be satisfied when your spirits are intertwined with a greater Spirit, Jesus Christ. So as you use this devotional, we pray that God's Son will dwell in your relationship richly.

—LES AND LESLIE PARROTT,
SEATTLE, WASHINGTON

Session One

LIVING HAPPILY EVER AFTER

The first apartment we had was so small that our prized possession, a hand-me-down king-sized bed with a matching chest of drawers and big-framed mirror, had to be put in the living area. The kitchen was so small it would only accommodate one of us at a time. The walls were so thin they were little more than a sight barrier to our neighbor, whose conversations could sometimes be monitored.

That was then; this is now. After ten years in one-bedroom apartments we now have our own house. It has a well-proportioned bedroom that holds our big bed and all the matching pieces. Our kitchen includes a cooking island large enough for both of us to prepare the food or clean the mess together. And the sounds of neighbors are too far away to matter.

So has it made a difference in our marriage? Are we happier now that we have accumulated more "stuff," or were we just as happy when we had next to nothing? In some ways we are happier now, or at least more relaxed. We no longer post the monthly income in twenty-dollar bills on the wall above the kitchen sink and visibly watch and pray for a twenty to be left over at the end of the month for some discretionary spending. We both work and we don't spend all we make. And to that extent, we are happier because of reduced financial anxiety.

But at this point in the maturation of our marriage, we've come to realize more and more that it is our relationship with each other that matters most, not the comfort and conveniences we have around us. No matter how much a couple has, they always believe a little bit more would be just enough. In fact, studies have shown that most couples believe they would be happier if their income were 20 percent higher. Of course, 20 percent more will never satisfy, at least not for long. As our increases are absorbed into the living standard, expectations rise and the cycle repeats itself.

Above a certain subsistence level which varies with the life stage of each couple, happiness in marriage depends on the quality of the relationship. And this is true at all stages of life, for richer, for poorer. The writer of Ecclesiastes says, "Better one handful with tranquillity than two handfuls with toil and chasing after the wind" (Eccl. 4:6; see also Prov. 15:17; 17:1).

So if you are living in a one-bedroom apartment praying that your monthly income will outlast the month, remember these wise words: "Do not wear yourself out to get rich; do not trust in your own cleverness. Cast but a glance at riches, and they are gone, for they will surely sprout wings and fly off to the sky like an eagle" (Prov. 23:4–5). It is far more rewarding to work at becoming soul mates. For the riches of a happy marriage will outlast all other possessions.

FROM GOD'S WORD

Command those who are rich in this present world not to be arrogant nor to put their hope in wealth, which is so uncertain, but to put their hope in God, who richly provides us with everything for our enjoyment. Command them to do good, to be rich in good deeds, and to be generous and willing to share. In this way they will lay up treasure for themselves as a firm foundation for the coming age, so that they may take hold of the life that is truly life.

1 Timothy 6:17–19

YOUR TURN

- Why would the passage from 1 Timothy warn against putting your hope in wealth? How does being "rich in good deeds" apply to marriage?
- Give an example of a time when you experienced peace and contentment in your marriage even in the absence of creature comforts. What made it so?
- If you are like most couples, you probably believe a little more income would make you a lot happier. What kinds of differences do you think you would notice?
- Do you agree with the writer of Ecclesiastes that "better [is] one handful with tranquillity than two . . . with toil"? If so, how are you applying that to your marriage relationship?
- In what practical ways are you investing in your marriage so that it will outlast material possessions?

SOUL TO SOUL

To deepen your spiritual intimacy this next week, make note of:

- What you gained from this session together.
- A pressure point in your partner's upcoming week you will pray about.
- A concrete kindness you can offer your partner this week.

PRAYER

Gracious God, thank you for our marriage. Thank you for the joy and happiness it brings to our lives. Teach us to realize that drawing our strength from you and learning to love one another is critical to our well-being. We long to be soul mates and ask you to teach us how. Amen.

Real-Life Soul Mates

I wasn't the brightest guy on the block when I married Sande, the woman who had captured my heart. But I did one thing right. After our lavish wedding, where we spent $29 on flowers, and our reception, which consisted of ham and cheese sandwiches at her aunt's home, we took off for Yuma, Arizona, in our un-air-conditioned 1960 Corvair. It was August and 105 degrees. Yet as soon as we left our well-wishers behind, I pulled that Corvair over to the side of the road.

There, in the sweltering heat, I prayed for us, our marriage, and that God would bless and unite us in every way possible. It was my first act as a husband and, I am convinced, my most important one. It started our marital journey off on the right foot. That act of spiritual intimacy formed our bond as solid cement, because God was the hardening agent.

We never wanted to do daily devotions together, but we did other traditional things, such as attending church and community Bible study. However, what grew our spiritual intimacy the most was talking about and observing God's mighty presence in nature. As we'd sit outside our summer home in New York with the moon shining on the lake, I'd say, "God did a pretty good job of hanging that moon in exactly the right place to reflect sunlight, didn't he?"

"Ohhh," she'd breathe, "and look at those stars. So many. And God knows them all by name. Just like he knows us by name."

Admiring nature helped us grasp the enormity of God—his power and detailed care in creating everything from centipedes to aardvarks to human beings. As our awe and respect for him grew, our spiritual intimacy leaped to new heights.

Today, over four decades later, Sande and I are living proof of that continual growth. Even more, we've had the tremendous privilege of passing that legacy to our five children and grandchildren. For us, the key to spiritual intimacy is simply this:

- Pray.
- Communicate.
- Look around at God's world.

You might be viewing the Grand Canyon, Mount Everest, or a single flower growing in the crack of a sidewalk. You might be admiring the moonlight and stars from the balcony of your apartment or your own backyard. If you do so, think of us. We'll be looking at the same radiant sky.

Now there's another miracle in itself.

Kevin and Sande Leman

DOUBLE YOUR SERVE

Dietrich Bonhoeffer, the German theologian who was hanged by the Nazis during World War II, wrote a wonderful wedding sermon while he was in prison, but he never had a chance to deliver it in person. He wrote:

> Marriage is more than your love for each other. It has a higher dignity and power, for it is God's holy ordinance. . . . In your love you see only the heaven of your happiness, but in marriage you are placed at a post of responsibility toward the world and mankind. Your love is your own private possession, but marriage is something more than personal—it is a status, an office . . . that joins you together in the sight of God.

Have you thought about the "higher dignity and power" of your marriage? We know of nothing else that can cultivate the intimacy of soul mates more than reaching out to the world as a team. Doing good for others as a couple brings a mystical quality into your marriage. It helps you transcend yourselves and become part of something larger.

God is committed to one major objective: helping us conform to the image of his Son (see Phil. 2:5–11). And his Son, Scripture says, came not to be served but to serve (Mark 10:45). It is as straightforward as that. God wants us to be a giving people. Philippians 2:4 says, " . . . not looking to your own interests, but each of you to the interests of the others." Galatians 5:13 says, "Serve one another in love."

Marriage is a great means to becoming more like Christ. Paul says to "spur one another on toward love and good deeds" (Heb. 10:24). Marriage helps us do just that, and when we join our efforts in service together we are doubly blessed.

There are literally hundreds of ways to incorporate shared service into your marriage—offering hospitality in your home, volunteering at a shelter, sponsoring a needy child, working in the church nursery. The key is to find something that fits your personal style. One of the ways we enjoy reaching out as a couple is by doing something anonymously. Even something small. We call it a mission of service in secret. It is an act of kindness that is concealed from everyone but the two of us. Our own sense of devotion and intimacy deepens as we secretly observe the results of our service.

Two people joined in marriage, as Bonhoeffer said, are ordained to serve others as a team. As a partnership, two people can serve other people better than they could as separate individuals. So don't neglect the practice of shared service. It will do more to enrich the soul of your marriage than you can ever imagine.

FROM GOD'S WORD

Whoever wants to become great among you must be your servant, and whoever wants to be first must be slave of all. For even the Son of Man did not come to be served, but to serve, and to give his life as a ransom for many.

MARK 10:43–45

YOUR TURN

- What role does shared service play in your spiritual journey together? Are you reaching out as a team the way you would like to?
- Give an example of how your partner has inspired you to do a specific good deed.
- In your opinion, how is intimacy in marriage linked to shared service?
- Bonhoeffer said that shared service gives your marriage "dignity and meaning." What does that mean to you?
- How can the two of you more effectively practice shared service in your marriage? What specific things might you do?

SOUL TO SOUL

To deepen your spiritual intimacy this next week, make note of:

- What you gained from this session together.
- A pressure point in your partner's upcoming week you will pray about.
- A concrete kindness you can offer your partner this week.

PRAYER

Dear God, reveal to us the higher dignity and power of our marriage. Teach us to spur one another on, gently and lovingly, toward becoming more like Christ. We want to double our efforts by serving you together as a team, so please help us discover our unique gift of shared service as a couple. We pray this sincerely. Amen.

Real-Life Soul Mates

In 2003, I spent ten days in Uganda, Africa. While on that trip I saw things that changed my entire view on life. I saw little children who were starving because of a lack of food and clean water. I returned home from that trip about mid-November, and as I was unpacking my oversized suitcase and placing unused items in a storage closet, I came across a box that had several Christmas gifts from the year before, unwrapped but still in the product packaging. Although we had spent hundreds of dollars on these gifts, they were so unnecessary they had managed to stay in that storage closet for almost an entire year. It almost made me sick. I had just left a village where kids were starving, and here I was, face-to-face with the reality of my excess. I had so much excess that the gifts that had seemed so important eleven and a half months earlier were literally rotting in my closet. What if we had simply donated the hundreds of dollars we had spent on these unneeded and never-used gifts to sponsor food for those kids? How many kids would still be alive?

Christmas was fast approaching, and the sobering reality of my wastefulness made me think. Up until now Christmas was all about me. What I wanted, what I would get, *my* gifts, *my* kids, *my* family, and eating *my* yummy food. After I got back from Africa, that egocentric, self-centered view of Christmas felt very wrong.

I resolved Christmas was going to be different. I was not going to buy into the materialism. I went to my husband Brice and told him of my idea of doing something completely different.

"You know what, Shelene, I love this," he responded. "Let's make this Christmas about somebody else. Besides, it's not your birthday; it's Jesus' birthday!"

That was the start of an amazing tradition in the Bryan family. For our family, Christmas morning is about serving other people. We have passed out Christmas flowers in a retirement home, where a woman who had not spoken a single word in several years was so touched she began to thank us out loud, to the shock of the nursing staff. We have visited sick children and sung Christmas carols at a children's hospital. For the past several years we have been the guest chefs at a homeless shelter. That always cracks me up because Brice and my kids have always teased me that the best thing I make is "reservations." But the shelter people always seem to enjoy the Christmas breakfast, never mind that the waffles are not perfectly fluffy and the bacon is slightly burnt. When we finally get back home to our own Christmas celebration, the joy that comes from serving others and the amazing conversations we have about the fascinating people we meet are times that have drawn us together as a couple and a family like nothing else.

Brice and Shelene Bryan

Session Three

ALL FOR A BAR OF SOAP

In *Love in the Time of Cholera*, Nobel laureate Gabriel Garcia Marquez portrays a marriage that disintegrates over a bar of soap. It was the wife's job to keep the house in order, including the towels, toilet paper, and soap in the bathroom. One day she forgot to replace the soap. Her husband exaggerated the oversight: "I've been bathing for almost a week without any soap." She vigorously denied forgetting to replace the soap. Although she had indeed forgotten, her pride was at stake, and she would not back down. For the next seven months they slept in separate rooms and ate in silence. Their marriage had suffered a heart attack.

"Even when they were old and placid," writes Marquez, "they were very careful about bringing it up, for the barely healed wounds could begin to bleed again as if they had been inflicted only yesterday." How can a bar of soap ruin a marriage? The answer is actually simple: Neither partner would say, "Forgive me."

Forgiveness is critically important to the success of marriage. In becoming soul mates you must wrap and rewrap your partnership over and over with many layers of forgiveness. Why, you ask? Because forgiveness is the only way to break the inevitable cycle of blame and pain in a marriage. Two people living together are going to, at some point, get on each other's nerves. A power struggle will emerge over a tit-for-tat issue: "I can't believe you didn't buy the cereal I like."

"Wait a minute, aren't you supposed to be in charge of the groceries?"

"Don't try to pass the blame to me—you said you would buy it."

"Yes, but I told you to remind me."

"Why should I? It's your responsibility."

Such inane conversation bleats on and on in marriage until one of the partners says, "I'm sorry. Will you forgive me?" Marriage cannot last without forgiveness. If you are looking for fairness, don't look for it in marriage. Soul mates survive on forgiveness, not fairness.

Forgiving your partner is a way of saying, "I'm human. I make mistakes. I want to be granted that privilege, and so I grant you that privilege." The fourth chapter of Hebrews makes explicit this mystery of incarnation on a higher level: "We do not have a high priest who is unable to empathize with our weaknesses, but we have one who has been tempted in every way, just as we are—yet he did not sin" (verse 15).

Charles Williams has suggested that "no word in English carries a greater possibility of terror than the little word *as* in 'forgive us our trespasses, as we forgive those who trespass against us.' For this clause in the Lord's Prayer tells us that 'the condition of forgiving then is to be forgiven; the condition of being forgiven is to forgive.'" So wrap your marriage in forgiveness. "Be kind and compassionate to one another, forgiving each other, just as in Christ God forgave you" (Eph. 4:32).

FROM GOD'S WORD

Therefore, as God's chosen people, holy and dearly loved, clothe yourselves with compassion, kindness, humility, gentleness and patience. Bear with each other and forgive one another if any of you has a grievance against someone. Forgive as the Lord forgave you. And over all these virtues put on love, which binds them all together in perfect unity.

COLOSSIANS 3:12–14

YOUR TURN

- Discuss the meaning of Christ's message about forgiveness in the Lord's Prayer and how it relates to your marriage.
- Give an example of a time when forgiveness broke the cycle of blame and pain in your marriage.
- Sometimes it is as difficult to ask for forgiveness as it is to grant it. How can each of you work on taking the initiative in this?
- Have you ever fallen into the trap of believing marriage is supposed to be fair? What allows you to make a shift from fairness to forgiveness in your marriage?
- What is one thing you can do to prepare in advance to face the next unfair situation with repentance and forgiveness between you?

SOUL TO SOUL

To deepen your spiritual intimacy this next week, make note of:

- What you gained from this session together.
- A pressure point in your partner's upcoming week you will pray about.
- A concrete kindness you can offer your partner this week.

PRAYER

Lord, save us from making major issues out of minor incidents. Teach us how to distinguish what is significant and what is not. Also, teach us to walk the path of forgiveness in our marriage. Weave repentance and forgiveness into the fabric of our marriage by your grace. Amen.

Real-Life Soul Mates

Heidi and I realized early in our marriage that a prerequisite to intimacy of any kind was a foundation of respect for each other and for our relationship. As a result we've tried to build and maintain what I've since referred to as a "Wall of Tenderness" designed to keep out destructive attitudes, while keeping us close to each other. This wall entails:

- Not discussing problems in harsh, angry tones, but in attentive conversation, while working toward solutions that genuinely satisfy both of us.
- Not joking cuttingly about each other, especially in front of others.
- Never kidding about divorce.
- Saving constructive criticism for when we're alone and in a receptive frame of mind.
- Being willing to give in to each other's preferences, and developing a language for conveying when that is really needed. Some friends encouraged us to reserve the simple phrase "this is really important to me" for those times when we most need to be heard and respected.
- Regularly giving verbal and nonverbal encouragement to each other for who we are as well as for what we do. This includes doing things that make the other person feel treasured, including dinner dates, gifts, messages, prayers, and time alone together without distractions.
- Fostering an attitude that says, in effect, "I'd rather die than hurt or bring shame on you. You're the one precious person to whom I've committed my love for the rest of my life."

These actions and attitudes have helped us to build a strong foundation for our marriage. We're thankful to say that after almost thirty-plus years together, we're still in love, still laughing together, still learning and growing together. And we're looking forward with anticipation to the next thirty years.

Mark and Heidi Mittelberg

LIGHTEN UP

We laugh a lot together. Not a day goes by, it seems, that one of us does not crack up the other one—on purpose or by accident. An unexpected expression, a mispronounced word, or a faux pas in front of others is all it takes to get us laughing. A line from a movie or sitcom that struck us funny will be repeated in our home for weeks. But every once in a while, usually in the midst of an intense and serious talk when one of us is not yet ready to play, a joke will backfire.

Humor is always risky. What is appealing to some is appalling to others. In a survey of over fourteen thousand *Psychology Today* readers who rated thirty jokes, the findings were unequivocal. "Every single joke," it was reported, "had a substantial number of fans who rated it 'very funny,' while another group dismissed it as 'not at all funny.'" Apparently, our funny bones are located in different places. Some laugh uproariously at the slapstick of Larry, Moe, and Curly, while others enjoy the more cerebral humor of Woody Allen.

We can't tell you exactly how to bring more laughter into your marriage; that's a matter of personal preference. But we can tell you that your marriage will benefit greatly from humor. Laughter has important physiological effects on you and your partner. The French philosopher Voltaire wrote, "The art of medicine consists of amusing the patient while nature cures the disease." Modern research indicates that people with a sense of humor have fewer symptoms of physical illness than those who are less humorous. This idea, however, is not new. Since King Solomon's time, people have known about and applied the healing benefits of humor. Proverbs 17:22 tells us, "A cheerful heart is good medicine."

In fact, the Bible as a whole reminds us again and again of the "sounds of joy and gladness" (Jer. 7:34). The book of Proverbs says that "the cheerful heart has a continual feast" (15:15). The psalmist sings, "Our mouths were filled with laughter" (126:2). Isaiah exults, "Shout for joy, you heavens; rejoice, you earth" (49:13). Jesus told his disciples that after he left them, "your grief will turn to joy . . . and no one will take away your joy" (John 16:20, 22). The apostle Peter confirms that the Christians to whom he is writing "are filled with an inexpressible and glorious joy" (1 Peter 1:8).

Humor helps us cope—not just with the trivial but even with the tragic. Martin Grotjahn, author of *Beyond Laughter*, notes that "to have a sense of humor is to have an understanding of human suffering." Charlie Chaplin could have said the same thing. Chaplin grew up in the poorest section of London. His mother suffered from serious mental illness and his father died of alcoholism when Charlie was just five. Laughter was Chaplin's tool for coping with life's losses.

It's been said that if you can find humor in a tough time, you can survive it. Researchers agree. Studies reveal that individuals who have a strong sense of humor are less likely to experience depression and other forms of mood disturbance.

So it is not surprising that humor is good for your marriage. To paraphrase the nineteenth-century minister Henry Ward Beecher, a marriage without a sense of humor is like a wagon without springs—jolted by every bump in the road. Do your marriage a favor. Smooth out the bumpy times with a little laughter.

FROM GOD'S WORD

Shout for joy to the LORD, all the earth. Worship the LORD with gladness; come before him with joyful songs.

PSALM 100:1–2

Rejoice in the Lord always. I will say it again: Rejoice!

PHILIPPIANS 4:4

YOUR TURN

- Jesus was accused by some of enjoying life too much! In your opinion, how does his life model humor and fun?
- What things make you laugh together? How is your sense of humor similar to or different from your partner's?
- Does your humor as a couple ever turn hurtful? If so, when are those times and how can they be prevented?
- Give an example of a time when your partner's sense of humor lifted you out of a dark mood or a worried frame of mind.
- What can you do this week to lighten up as a couple?

SOUL TO SOUL

To deepen your spiritual intimacy this next week, make note of:

- What you gained from this session together.
- A pressure point in your partner's upcoming week you will pray about.
- A concrete kindness you can offer your partner this week.

PRAYER

Gracious God, we thank you for the healing gift of laughter and ask you to help us to laugh together often. Teach us to see ourselves in the light of eternity and laugh at what might otherwise bring worry or self-reproach. Fill us with your joy and bind us together with cheerful hearts. Amen.

Real-Life Soul Mates

We were high school sweethearts. When we first met, she literally fell at my feet! I attribute that to my stunning good looks, but she claims she tripped over her friend's foot. Anyway, that was the beginning of our love journey. Shortly thereafter, my wife began attending the Bible club that I established in our high school. During our high school years we also met a couple of times a week for early-morning prayer before school.

Though more than thirty years have passed since that time, we are still finding joy in the journey together! We are different people, with different likes and dislikes. Yet we find great joy in being connected through our relationships with God and family. We have five children and four grandchildren, and spending time with our family connects our hearts even more. If one of our children experienced a challenge, my wife and I would pray separately to seek the Lord for direction. Although we prayed in two separate places, we were reaching out to the same Lord. And each time, God essentially gave us virtually the same answer. That always amazed both of us.

In our journey, we sometimes go on long walks together in the morning, sharing our hearts with one another and discussing new insights that we receive from our Bible reading. Other mornings, we work out at the gym together, chatting with each other on the elliptical machines. Yet other times we connect by riding our bicycles on a trail. I'm always amazed how routinely doing physical activity together has deepened a spiritual bond between us. We have found ourselves experiencing the holy while doing the mundane. Sometimes we are making fresh vegetable juice together or cooking a meal together, but our hearts are always ultimately turned toward God.

We've always both loved humor. We cannot tell you how many times humor has diverted what could have turned into an argument! But instead we both end up laughing our way into wholeness and happiness. When my father was in the hospital facing a rare and dangerous operation, I called my husband on the phone. Just hearing his voice brought peace to my heart and confirmed that the decision we were making was the right thing to do. The operation was a success, and peace prevailed.

We both eventually lost our dads, but we've never been forsaken by our heavenly Father! Our resolve is to love, listen, learn, laugh, and leave a legacy.

Dale and Nina Bronner

Session Five

YOUR MONEY MATTERS

"Why do you always make the money decisions?" I asked. Les and I were standing in the middle of a department store trying to choose a new couch for our apartment. And it seemed to me that he was controlling the purse strings.

"I don't make the money decisions," he said, "our bank account does." That remark was followed by a lengthy, whiny discussion—okay, it was a fight—over how we manage, or should manage, our money. Was *he* in charge or were *we* in charge? Some of our biggest fights are financially focused.

Money, of course, has always provided plenty of fodder for marital discord. It is, after all, the most common source of conflict between couples. And with good reason. The dollar serves as a weapon of independence. It provides a battleground for disputes over responsibility and judgment. Financial issues can even be a forum for airing doubts about self-worth. A partner who is financially irresponsible, for example, may be broadcasting a message: Rescue me, solve my problems. A spouse's reluctance to accept gifts may hide a deeper lack of trust. A woman who goes on a spending spree every time her husband becomes cold and withdrawn may be trying to get his attention.

When money problems regularly erupt into shouting matches or hurt feelings, it may be time to seek professional help. But if you are simply trying to avoid the embarrassment of raising your voice in a furniture store, here are some suggestions from experts for trying to work things out on your own. First, educate your spouse about your own money upbringing. Talk over financial matters regularly, at a time when money decisions are not pressing. And if one person pays the bills, he or she should tell the other partner where their money is going and when. And finally, agree on and write down your financial goals, short term and long term.

It is hard for most couples to talk about money. Yet Jesus spoke about money more frequently than any other subject except the kingdom of God. His careful attention to financial issues is one of the truly amazing things about the Gospel narratives. The range of his concern is startling: from the parable of the sower (Matt. 13:22) to the parable of the rich farmer (Luke 12:16–21), from the encounter with the rich young ruler (Matt. 19:21) to the encounter with Zacchaeus (Luke 19), from teachings on trust in the sixth chapter of Matthew to teachings on the danger of wealth in the sixth chapter of Luke.

Behind money are invisible spiritual powers, powers that seduce and deceive. Paul saw this fact when he observed that "the love of money is a root of all kinds of evils" (1 Tim. 6:10). Every marriage must build a fortress against these beguiling forces.

FROM GOD'S WORD

Do not store up for yourselves treasures on earth, where moths and vermin destroy, and where thieves break in and steal. But store up for yourselves treasures in heaven, where moths and vermin do not destroy, and where thieves do not break in and steal. For where your treasure is, there your heart will be also.

MATTHEW 6:19–21

YOUR TURN

- Discuss the meaning of Christ's message about money from Matthew 6:19–21 and how it relates to Paul's warning against the love of money in 1 Timothy 6:10.
- Give an example from your upbringing that illustrates your attitude toward money management.
- What are the financial goals you share as a couple, and how are you working to meet them?
- Most marriages have a "spender" and a "keeper." Talk about your roles and how each of you can learn from the other.
- How can the two of you prepare in advance to make your next money conflict less troublesome?

SOUL TO SOUL

To deepen your spiritual intimacy this next week, make note of:

- What you gained from this session together.
- A pressure point in your partner's upcoming week you will pray about.
- A concrete kindness you can offer your partner this week.

PRAYER

Loving God, help us to keep money in perspective. While it often seems we do not have enough, save us from taking our financial frustrations out on each other. And guide us in every financial decision. Help us be mature and responsible with the resources you have provided us. Amen.

Real-Life Soul Mates

Sharon and I have been married for more than thirty years, and we're both task-oriented people. We figured out a long time ago that our spirits most often come together when we're tackling things that need to be done.

That usually happens during our time together each morning. We have a date on our back deck every day at 5 a.m. We spend that time reflecting on Scripture, praying, and talking over coffee. For us, there's nothing better than spending time with God and each other as we watch the sun come up over the Tennessee hills.

So what do we talk about during those times to strengthen our relationship? The answer might surprise you: our budget and our calendars.

I know that sounds a little boring, and I admit it's not what you'd call romantic. But we honestly connect best when we openly and intentionally communicate about those two things.

Now, the first one probably isn't a big shock, right? After all, everybody knows Dave and Sharon Ramsey live on a budget! But it's more than two people just *doing* a budget together. It's the power of *agreeing* on a budget together as husband and wife.

When our spirits agree on our spending—especially in the area of giving—we connect on so many other points in our lives. Those conversations really do sweeten our relationship and help us grow spiritually.

And since we're both really busy, keeping our calendars in sync makes a huge difference too. We have to plan our time for each other and for our family. And with our crazy schedules, we have to make sure we're on the same page and moving in the same direction.

Jesus said, "Where your treasure is, there your heart will be also" (Luke 12:34). Our time and our money are just two of the treasures God has given us, and how we use them says a lot about our hearts—and our relationship.

To get the relationship right, we have to use the treasure right. And we've found that working together on our budget and our calendars actually draws us together in ways we never would have imagined when we were younger.

Like I said, it may not seem romantic, but it's carried us through our toughest patches in life. More importantly, it's made us better people and better spouses.

Dave and Sharon Ramsey

IN THE BEGINNING . . . GOD CREATED SEX!

So, how's your sex life? That's a fair question, isn't it? After all, sexuality is not a given, something that somehow miraculously takes care of itself once we enter marriage. It needs nurture, tenderness, education, and—are you ready for this?—religion.

It's a fact. Religion, according to some studies, is good for your sex life. As strange as it may sound, there is a strong link in marriage between spirituality and sexuality. Married couples who cultivate spiritual intimacy are far more likely to report higher satisfaction with their sex life than other couples.

This fact makes sense if you think about it. The mysteries, wonders, and pleasures of sex in marriage are a divine gift to celebrate. Scripture—right from the beginning—enthusiastically affirms sex within the bond of marriage.

Start with the first chapter of the Bible. It contains a magnificent comment on the meaning of sexuality in marriage. As God is bringing the universe into existence we are told that the human creation is set apart from all others, for it is the *imago Dei*, the image of God: "So God created mankind in his own image, in the image of God he created them; male and female he created them" (Gen. 1:27). Our maleness and femaleness is not just an accidental arrangement of the human species. Our male and female sexuality is related to our creation in the image of God. This point is echoed throughout Scripture.

Consider the Song of Songs. Karl Barth has called the Song an expanded commentary on Genesis 2:25—"Adam and his wife were both naked, and they felt no shame." If Genesis affirms our sexuality, the Song of Songs celebrates it. There is no other portion of Scripture that is more extravagant. The Song of Songs describes sensuality without licentiousness, passion without promiscuity, love without lust.

In the New Testament, Paul quotes the Genesis passage about the husband leaving father and mother and cleaving to his wife so that the two become one flesh, and then he adds: "This is a profound mystery—but I am talking about Christ and the church" (Eph. 5:32).

Jesus, likewise, underscores a high view of sex in marriage. He refers to the Genesis passage and then adds, "So they are no longer two, but one flesh. Therefore what God has joined together, let no one separate" (Matt. 19:6).

The Old Testament and the New Testament, the Gospels and the Epistles, call us to celebrate sexuality in marriage. There is no denying that your spiritual growth helps to enhance your sexual intimacy in marriage. So, we'll ask it again. How's your sex life?

FROM GOD'S WORD

Then the Lord God made a woman from the rib he had taken out of the man, and he brought her to the man. The man said, "This is now bone of my bones and flesh of my flesh; she shall be called 'woman,' for she was taken out of man." That is why a man leaves his father and mother and is united to his wife, and they become one flesh. Adam and his wife were both naked, and they felt no shame.

GENESIS 2:22–25

YOUR TURN

- Discuss the link between spirituality and sexuality. How would each of you articulate this connection? How could your sex life be a barometer of your spiritual health as a couple?
- Give an example from your early years that illustrates how you were educated about sex.
- One place in marriage where we want to keep the mystery, excitement, and fascination is in sexual intimacy. Talk about what you could do as a couple to avoid falling into a boring routine.
- Talk about how the two of you initiate sexual intimacy in your marriage. How could your times of lovemaking be better for each of you?
- How could the two of you more effectively celebrate the gift of sex in marriage?

SOUL TO SOUL

To deepen your spiritual intimacy this next week, make note of:

- What you gained from this session together.
- A pressure point in your partner's upcoming week you will pray about.
- A concrete kindness you can offer your partner this week.

PRAYER

Gracious God, you have enthusiastically affirmed the gift of our shared sexuality and have created us with an unfathomable capacity for intimacy and pleasure. Dwell in our marriage—enhance our oneness in body and soul. Amen.

Real-Life Soul Mates

Ashley and I have always believed that the key to real intimacy in marriage is nakedness, so we decided early on that we wanted to have a lifelong "Naked Marriage."

You might be thinking I'm just talking about sex or maybe some kind of weird nudist colony, but I'm talking about something else entirely. Yes, sex is a huge part of marriage, and you should make it a priority, but a "Naked Marriage" doesn't just refer to physical nakedness.

When God created the first married couple in the Garden of Eden, they were both naked, but they had no shame (see Gen. 2:25). That nakedness paints a vivid picture of the physical and sexual intimacy between a husband and wife, but God was also painting a picture of the emotional and spiritual nakedness that must be present in marriage.

God was using nakedness to illustrate the complete honesty, complete transparency, complete vulnerability, and complete acceptance between a husband and a wife. This means a husband and wife must be able to stand before each other with nothing to hide.

In our marriage, we put this into practice in many ways, and one of the most practical is our "Secret-Free Guarantee." In order to have complete honesty in marriage, we know there can be no room for secrets. There are no hidden passwords, bank accounts, text messages, or anything else that would be "off limits" to each other.

Unless we're hiding a Christmas gift or planning a surprise birthday party, there's absolutely no room for secrets in marriage. Secrecy is the enemy of intimacy. We've recognized that the level of our honesty will always determine the level of our intimacy.

The second way we put this into practice is through regular communication. We've found that communication does for a marriage what breathing does for a body. We talk and text throughout the day, and we try to carve out some uninterrupted time for conversation after the kids are asleep each night. Conversation cultivates intimacy.

A third way we put this into practice is by actually being naked as often as possible. This one is my favorite! You should give it a try. It was God's idea, so you know it works.

Dave and Ashley Willis

Session Seven

CARING ENOUGH
TO COMMIT

"It is easier in these United States to walk away from a marriage than from a commitment to purchase a used car," said an attorney at a conference we attended. "Most contracts cannot be unilaterally terminated. A marriage commitment, however, can be broken by practically anyone at any time, and without cause."

He is right. A friend of ours who went to traffic court heard two divorce decrees from the judge before his turn came to be heard. He dropped by our office later to tell us about his experience. He said, "I told my wife when I got home that we could have had a divorce any number of times if those reasons I heard in court were good enough for a legal separation."

A few decades back, this wasn't so. In those days, many had to travel to Mexico or acquire residency in Nevada in order to obtain a divorce. Others had to make believe that one of the parties had engaged in a nefarious affair. Contemporary America concluded that marital bonds were tied too tightly and responded with no-fault divorce. A generation later, the value of marriage has dwindled significantly.

The "till death do us part" of marriage, however, is not an ideal but a reality ensured by an unswerving commitment—a willful agreement to keep love alive. "Do two walk together unless they have agreed to do so?" asked the prophet Amos (3:3). Commitment is the cerebral part of love, the part that comes more from our mind than our heart.

Why do so many marriage commitments fall flat these days? We believe it is because too many promises are made without the promises of God. We can "hold unswervingly to the hope we profess, for he who promised is faithful" (Heb. 10:23). Our commitment to each other in marriage is sustained by God's model of faithfulness to us. When a man and woman covenant with one another, God promises faithfulness to them (see 1 Cor. 1:9). There is no way to overemphasize the centrality of commitment in God's character. It is woven into every part of the Bible—from Genesis, where God initiates his promise of faithfulness, through Revelation, where John's vision depicts "a white horse, whose rider is called Faithful and True" (19:11).

Today's covenant, embodied in our partner, makes a home for our restless hearts. It accepts our whole soul by saying, "I believe in you and commit myself to you through thick and thin." Without commitment and the trust it engenders, marriage would have no hope of enduring. For no couple can achieve deep confidence in their own fidelity until they first recognize God's faithfulness to them.

FROM GOD'S WORD

Know therefore that the Lord your God is God; he is the faithful God, keeping his covenant of love to a thousand generations of those who love him and keep his commandments.

DEUTERONOMY 7:9

YOUR TURN

- Commitment is essential to knowing who God is. How would you describe this quality of God to a person who does not know him? What biblical examples and personal experiences would you use to illustrate God's commitment?

- Give an example of how God's commitment to you has been realized in your life.
- Some people are pessimistic about lifelong marriage. They have seen too many marriages fail. What makes you believe your marriage will be "till death do us part"?
- Commitment stems from a conscious decision. What are you doing to reaffirm this decision in your marriage? How is your commitment expressed?
- If someone were observing your marriage for signs of commitment, what would they take note of?

SOUL TO SOUL

To deepen your spiritual intimacy this next week, make note of:

- What you gained from this session together.
- A pressure point in your partner's upcoming week you will pray about.
- A concrete kindness you can offer your partner this week.

PRAYER

Gracious God, we thank you for the privilege of entering this lifelong pilgrimage of marriage together. We know that it is only through commitment that our relationship will be sustained, so we ask you to strengthen our commitment daily. And help us to express our commitment that we might be buoyed by one another's holy pledge. Amen.

Real-Life Soul Mates

Kate and I recently celebrated our ten-year anniversary with a trip to Europe. One day we rented a canoe to go down a lazy river in a beautiful valley full of medieval castles. We were told that no one ever falls into this river because the water is so calm, so we were fully dressed and ready for the relaxing ride.

About fifteen minutes into our romantic voyage I unscrewed the top of our waterproof container (why did we even need that thing?) and took out Kate's camera to take some pictures. I didn't bother to screw the lid back on the bucket that also contained Kate's purse and our lunch.

Well, we must have been the first people to encounter that river's only rapid. Kate will tell you that I catapulted her out of the canoe, but all I remember is losing my balance in the back of the boat and watching as my wife went headfirst into the water followed by me, followed by our belongings, which all floated downstream.

After the shock that we'd actually fallen in wore off a bit, we started to be more intentional about paddling as a team, keeping our balance, and staying in the center of the boat. In fact, when one of us would start to lean to one side a little too much, the other would call out, "Stay centered!" We certainly didn't want to be the only people to ever fall into that river twice, and we had four hours of paddling to go!

As we've talked about it, that canoe ride was a great metaphor for our spiritual journey together in marriage. We love just spending time together, and we could float along pretty happily without paddling, but our marriage definitely works best when we're each intentional about pursuing God.

Our spiritual strengths are different—Kate is definitely more consistent with Bible reading, for instance, but she's also great about sharing with me what she learns while I share with her from the many sermons and podcasts that I listen to while I travel. Along the same lines, writing music is a spiritual practice for me whereas Kate chooses to journal. We don't have to do the same things together all the time to maintain spiritual intimacy. But when rough waters come, being grounded by our individual spiritual practices helps us navigate better together.

We also share great spiritual time together (like a sermon that we can't stop talking about, an eye-opening devotional, or a powerful prayer time), and it's like we're paddling in perfect synchronization. At other times, one of us is spiritually weak and the other person has to paddle a little more. Regardless of where we are in the journey, though, we've learned the importance of the simple phrase "Stay centered." It's a reminder for each of us to keep God in the center of the boat, know that we'll fall overboard sometimes, but hopefully laugh about it farther downstream.

Mark and Kate Schultz

TURNING "ME" TO "WE"

In the center of your head is a structure of the brain whose purpose is survival. It is the intensive care unit of the nervous system, the part of the supersystem that helps you stay well. This part of the brain, called the limbic system, is consumed with either fighting, fleeing, or feeding. Body temperature, heartbeat, breathing, sweating, and the general response of the body to the world begin here.

The limbic system reacts to any change in our internal or external world, a type of biological Geiger counter. But it does not read, consider, evaluate, or assess in terms of the welfare of the world. It is only concerned with survival. Unless told otherwise, there is no "us" in the lower levels of the brain, only "self."

In 2 Timothy 3:2–4, Paul came up with a frightening list describing the self-centered person: "People will be lovers of themselves, lovers of money, boastful, proud, abusive, disobedient to their parents, ungrateful, unholy, without love, unforgiving, slanderous, without self-control, brutal, not lovers of the good, treacherous, rash, conceited, lovers of pleasure rather than lovers of God."

None of us could abide marriage with the person described by Paul. In fact, there are laws to protect us from such persons. But according to Galatians 5:22, no law can bring about the qualities that transcend a selfish focus on "me." These qualities are the fruit of inviting the Holy Spirit to transform our self-centered tendencies. They include love, goodness, joy, faithfulness, peace, gentleness, patience, self-control, and kindness.

What person would not like to make a home with the partner who demonstrates these qualities? These are the marks of the individual who has transcended selfishness and turned "me" into "we." Every marriage runs the risk of becoming two self-centered persons consumed, like the limbic system, with individual survival. But when the Holy Spirit is allowed to transform our self-gratifying nature, the real miracle of marriage occurs: The more we give of ourselves, the more fruit we enjoy.

FROM GOD'S WORD

For the entire law is fulfilled in keeping this one command: "Love your neighbor as yourself." If you bite and devour each other, watch out or you will be destroyed by each other. So I say, walk by the Spirit, and you will not gratify the desires of the flesh. For the flesh desires what is contrary to the Spirit, and the Spirit what is contrary to the flesh. They are in conflict with each other, so that you are not to do whatever you want. But if you are led by the Spirit, you are not under the law.

GALATIANS 5:14–18

YOUR TURN

- In your experience, how does the work of the Holy Spirit enable us to transcend self-centeredness?
- Give an example of a time when you set aside selfish concerns to be more loving toward your partner. Looking

back, can you see any fruit that your choice produced in your marriage?

- In what concrete ways is your life more "whole" now that you are married?
- When is the "individual survival mode" most likely to dominate your relationship? Give specific examples.
- Discuss in specific terms how you can work together to turn the balance of your marriage into a "we"-centered relationship.

SOUL TO SOUL

To deepen your spiritual intimacy this next week, make note of:

- What you gained from this session together.
- A pressure point in your partner's upcoming week you will pray about.
- A concrete kindness you can offer your partner this week.

PRAYER

Heavenly Father, it is your Spirit dwelling in our marriage that enables us to transcend our self-concern and more effectively love one another. Reveal to us the power of this principle to produce a fruitful, thriving, and enjoyable marriage. Strengthen us by your grace to be a partner characterized by all the fruit of your Spirit. Amen.

Real-Life Soul Mates

We are convinced that our spiritual intimacy is a reflection of the love we share. Whether it is taking a walk, holding hands in front of the fire, or talking about God's movement in our lives, our relational commitment and intimacy is at the heart of who we are as individuals called to marriage. Though sometimes we wander off from each other, our journey in friendship and respect over the past thirty-five years has deepened our experience of life in Christ as a couple.

We have few "spiritual rituals," unless you can call a commitment to weekly dates, quarterly getaways, and spontaneous romantic interludes "spiritual rituals." We do pray together, but our prayer life is more of an extension of the intimacy we share rather than an ordered, systematic formula. We often discuss Scripture, but instead of feeling forced, it comes from the passion of God's presence and conviction of God's prompting in our lives.

This is spiritual intimacy in marriage—two children on a walk through life, each holding the hand of the One who walks with them, savoring his companionship along the way.

Chap and Dee Clark

Session Nine

WHAT A DIFFERENCE A TEMPERAMENT MAKES!

After the great writer F. Scott Fitzgerald died, the executor of his estate found his notes on a play that was never written. The plot involved five members of one family who lived apart but would inherit a stately mansion if they could agree to only one condition—to live in the house together.

Marriage is a little like that unfinished play. People who have been living apart are suddenly offered life's most compelling rewards if they can only learn how to live together.

The catch, of course, is that living together is not always easy. It requires maturity. Some have suggested that two strangers could be married to each other off the street and make a pretty good marriage together if only they were mature enough to work their way through the inevitable differences.

How do you and your partner handle differences? If you are like most couples you probably try one of two things: You either sweep your differences under the rug by ignoring them altogether, or you try to make your partner become like yourself. Unfortunately, both strategies are doomed to frustration. For one thing, it is only a matter of time before repressed differences reemerge, and second, we miss out on a tremendous gift of marriage when we do not enjoy our partner's uniqueness. That's right, enjoy the differences!

In Psalm 139:14 we read, "I praise you because I am fearfully and wonderfully made; your works are wonderful, I know that full well." Every person is unique. God never intended couples to approach life as if they were twins separated at birth. He made us with unique strengths and weaknesses. He gave each of us special gifts.

The New Testament uses the image of a human body to illustrate the church (see 1 Cor. 12:12). A body composed of many members with many gifts can accomplish far more than a one-celled organism. The same principle applies to marriage. The differences in temperament that allow your partner to deal with situations that would drive you crazy is something to be thankful for. Sure, some of his or her traits make living together tough at times, but appreciating the positive side of your differences will make your marriage more balanced and complete. And like the family in Fitzgerald's unfinished play, you will inherit the riches only soul mates enjoy.

FROM GOD'S WORD

If you have any encouragement from being united with Christ, if any comfort from his love, if any common sharing in the Spirit, if any tenderness and compassion, then make my joy complete by being like-minded, having the same love, being one in spirit and of one mind. Do nothing out of selfish ambition or vain conceit. Rather, in humility value others above yourselves, not looking to your own interests but each of you to the interests of others.

PHILIPPIANS 2:1–4

YOUR TURN

- How do you and your partner handle differences? How could you improve the way you do this?
- Give an example of a time when your partner allowed the gift of your uniqueness to be evident in your marriage— a time when your differences were appreciated.
- How do you see the diversity of the body of Christ reflected in your marriage? In other words, how do your gifts differ from and complement one another?
- Discuss the tendency married people have to either sweep differences under the rug or try to change their partner. Where do you each fall on this continuum?
- What specific traits do each of you bring that create balance and completion in your marriage?

SOUL TO SOUL

To deepen your spiritual intimacy this next week, make note of:

- What you gained from this session together.
- A pressure point in your partner's upcoming week you will pray about.
- A concrete kindness you can offer your partner this week.

PRAYER

God of creation, teach us how to deal with the inevitable differences that are a part of marriage. Allow us to be grateful for these differences even when they first appear to be the source of our frustration. Help us to see that our individual characteristics bring fullness to our marriage, and grant us the courage to acknowledge and value our differences. Amen.

Real-Life Soul Mates

We come out on opposite poles in every category of personality assessments, whether it's extrovert and introvert or anything else. In fact, we are actually extreme opposites on all personality dimensions.

So that's fun.

But truth be told, our radical differences make for great adventures as well as great challenges.

We met in high school and began dating when we were sixteen years old. Our spiritual lives had a common goal but a different starting place.

Donna is more reflective and private in her prayer life, preferring to engage in solitary exercises of prayer and thoughtful meditation. Ed, on the other hand, engages with others. He prefers small groups where he can wrestle through Scripture and pray aloud in community. So even our spiritual lives are birthed from a different starting point.

However, what keeps us together is not the starting point of our personalities but the ending point of our common conviction. Two people of very different backgrounds or personalities, if headed in the same direction, actually grow closer to one another over time.

And so it's been with us. Over time we've grown to know and love one another more deeply each year. But the common thing between us has not been personality types, or hobbies we enjoy, or things we want to do together, but rather a relationship that's built first and foremost on a relationship with Jesus Christ.

Now, we don't want to give the impression that this is all ice cream and roses. The reality is there are certain things about each of us that we had to accept.

Donna needs peace and quiet. Ed needs lively interaction. Ed is more directional with the kids. Donna is more connectional with them.

The key for us is to acknowledge the differences. The differences don't go away, of course, and, yes, they are sometimes challenging. However, the differences become opportunities to learn. We can even begin to enjoy the differences, growing closer as we pursue our common direction and purpose.

Ed and Donna Stetzer

Session Ten

IF YOU BUGGED YOURSELF, WHAT WOULD YOU HEAR?

Some scientists in Great Britain have come up with the idea that every word that has ever been spoken is still floating around out there somewhere in space. All we need, they say, is one more scientific breakthrough and we can bring in any conversation that has ever occurred. We can hear Lincoln give his Gettysburg Address, or Caesar deliver his orations in the halls of the senate in Rome. We could even hear the words of our Lord as he gave the Sermon on the Mount.

But think of the personal implications. What if our conversations could be replayed at will? What if your partner could say, "Let's listen to what you said last Tuesday about that topic"?

Have you ever listened to yourself on tape? As counselors in training, each of us had to record our counseling sessions and play them back with our supervisors. It's an educational but nerve-wracking experience. The supervisor plays the tape for a few minutes, then hits the pause button: "There, did you notice what you just said?"

Thank goodness no one has played back what we say to each other in our own homes. But researchers at Duke University have recorded conversations in other homes. For six weeks they surreptitiously taped family conversations over mealtimes. After tabulating the results, they discovered that most conversations can be categorized in one of five ways: (1) non-conversations, (2) critical-of-family conversations, (3) critical-of-others conversations, (4) materialistic conversations, and (5) discussions of issues and ideas.

If you bugged yourself, if you recorded the conversations between you and your partner, what would you hear? What category of conversation would top your list?

The prophet Isaiah didn't have the technical equipment for recording his conversations in ancient Jerusalem, but when he was only twenty-six years of age he took a personal inventory of his talk. And what he found didn't please him: "Woe to me . . . I am ruined! For I am a man of unclean lips, and I live among a people of unclean lips, and my eyes have seen the King, the LORD Almighty" (Isa. 6:5).

Isaiah recognized negativism in himself. And like you and me, he could have easily justified it. He was at a low point in his life: Everything had fallen to pieces with the death of the king and the failure of the regime that followed. Isaiah had plenty of personal disappointments to cope with. He could have fortified his negative attitude with his friends; they certainly would have fanned the flame of a critical conversation. But Isaiah chose a different route. And God met his need with a live coal "which he had taken with tongs from the altar. With it he touched my mouth and said, 'See, this has touched your lips; your guilt is taken away and your sin atoned for'" (Isa.6:6–7).

The things you choose to talk about will determine the tone of your marriage—whether it is upbeat or colored by negativism. So ask yourself, what would you hear if your conversations were recorded?

FROM GOD'S WORD

When we put bits into the mouths of horses to make them obey us, we can turn the whole animal. Or take ships as an example. Although they are so large and are driven by strong winds, they are steered by a very small rudder wherever the pilot wants to go. Likewise, the tongue is a small part of the body, but it makes great boasts. Consider what a great forest is set on fire by a small spark. The tongue also is a fire, a world of evil among the parts of the body. It corrupts the whole body, sets the whole course of one's life on fire, and is itself set on fire by hell. . . . With the tongue we praise our Lord and Father, and with it we curse human beings, who have been made in God's likeness. Out of the same mouth come praise and cursing. My brothers and sisters, this should not be.

James 3:3–6, 9–10

YOUR TURN

- How is the topic of our conversations related to our spiritual journey?
- Give an example of a conversation topic that you and your partner sometimes focus on that is not healthy or productive.
- If you recorded a typical conversation between you and your partner over dinner, what would you hear? What topics come up most often?
- What type of conversation would your hear most often in the family you grew up in (critical of family, critical of others, materialistic, or issues and ideas)?
- What practical things can you do as a couple to avoid negative conversations?

SOUL TO SOUL

To deepen your spiritual intimacy this next week, make note of:

- What you gained from this session together.
- A pressure point in your partner's upcoming week you will pray about.
- A concrete kindness you can offer your partner this week.

PRAYER

Heavenly Father, thank you for the gift of communication. Help us to use it well. Keep us from allowing negativism to poison our conversations. Teach us to communicate wisely, conveying hope and encouragement to each other daily. Amen.

Real-Life Soul Mates

Before we ever walked down the aisle, we'd been preparing for unity in our marriage. How? By making a commitment to stand on the Word of God no matter what.

When we speak on marriage to couples, people will ask us how we keep the "spark" alive in our marriage. But I think we overemphasize the spark and underemphasize the fire we need to build over the years of marriage. It isn't just about what you feel. Feelings come and go. But when you work to honor each other, the blaze of affection grows.

So how do we do this in practical terms?

To start with, Brandy and I have a standing lunch date every single week. It takes priority over everything else. No kids and no phones are allowed. We laugh, eat, talk, and listen to each other. We see each other, eye-to-eye, without distractions.

We've seen too many marriages fail because the couple swept tough conversations under the rug for years. That's why we sometimes talk about tough issues at our weekly lunch. We work through our differences together. And without that standing lunch date, there's a pretty good chance those conversations would never happen. And when we struggle, we go to God's Word.

We also have quarterly getaways, and every year for the last several years we have taken an annual trip together. One year recently, I decided I didn't want to spend the money on the trip. It was a great business decision and a terrible relational decision—we haven't missed one since. These times together are essential for us to build the covenant we created when God joined us together.

When Brandy and I were engaged, she gave me a Bible that I still study out of every day. Inside she wrote the following: "I pray that our marriage will be a blessing not only to others, but also to God. As long as Jesus is the Lord of our relationship and we live by the standards set forth in his Word, our marriage will be successful and blessed."

Twenty years later I can say with confidence that we are more blessed than we could have ever imagined. This is our hope for you—that you may be richly blessed and may bless others in your marriage by standing on the unshakable Word of God.

Jeff and Brandy Little

Session Eleven

SLOPPY AGAPE

In the early days of aviation, pilots often used a phrase which described the nature of their work: "Flying by the seat of your pants." Before sophisticated instruments were as widely available on planes as they are today, the only guide for air navigation in inclement weather was pure physical sensation. If the pilot felt pressure from the seat of the aircraft, it probably meant he was ascending, much the same as the feeling you get in a rising elevator. Conversely, if there was a sensation of weightlessness, it most likely meant the plane was on the descent. This means flying, of course, was not reliable. In fact it was flat-out dangerous. Men met their deaths because their feelings played tricks on their judgment.

Feelings can be just as deadly when they are used to navigate your way through a marriage. Jan, married only a couple of years to Mike, came to us because she could never seem to please him.

"I'm not blaming Mike," Jan confided, "I just wish I could be a better wife. I do a lot for him, but it never seems to be enough." Jan took all the responsibility for Mike's happiness. And if he was not perfectly content—it was her fault!

Jan's marital happiness was at the mercy of her feelings. What's wrong with that? Well, when we use feelings to steer our marriage, we end up doing loving things rather than being a loving person. We end up falling into a trap we call "sloppy agape."

63

This kind of love can look like the ultimate in selflessness, but it continually misses the mark. A classic biblical example of sloppy agape is found in Jesus' friend Martha. They first met when Martha opened her home to Jesus and his disciples. Martha scurried about making preparations to serve the men, while her sister, Mary, simply sat and conversed with Jesus.

Finally, Martha complained, "Lord, don't you care that my sister has left me to do the work by myself? Tell her to help me!"

"Martha, Martha," the Lord answered. "You are worried and upset about many things, but few things are needed—or indeed only one. Mary has chosen what is better, and it will not be taken away from her" (Luke 10:40–42).

Martha was more concerned with doing loving things in the kitchen than being a loving person in her relationship with Jesus. She was attending to everyone else's needs, but she did not recognize her own need to sit at the feet of Jesus. Only later, when her faith in Jesus had grown, was she able to put aside her own worries and trust him even in the worst of circumstances—when her beloved brother, Lazarus, had died.

Don't get caught in the sloppy agape trap. If you focus too much on your feelings you will end up meeting needs your partner doesn't really have. Scurrying around and desperately trying to please your partner will only lead to disappointment on both sides. So if you rely too much on your feelings, remember to focus not just on doing loving things but on being a loving person.

FROM GOD'S WORD

If I speak in the tongues of men or of angels, but do not have love, I am only a resounding gong or a clanging cymbal. If I have the gift of prophecy and can fathom all mysteries and all knowledge, and if I have a faith that can move mountains, but do not have love, I am nothing. If I give all I possess to the poor and give over my body to hardship that I may boast, but do not have love, I gain nothing.

1 CORINTHIANS 13:1–3

YOUR TURN

- How have you allowed feelings to dictate your approach to marriage? Be specific.
- Give an example of a time when you met a need of your partner's out of a compulsion to please or simply to feel like a loving person. Did it backfire?
- Discuss how you can support one another in activities that meet your deepest spiritual needs.
- How can you distinguish between your partner's feelings and his or her genuine needs? Discuss what signs to look for in each other.
- What practical things can you do as a couple to encourage a focus on being loving persons rather than doing loving things?

SOUL TO SOUL

To deepen your spiritual intimacy this next week, make note of:

- What you gained from this session together.
- A pressure point in your partner's upcoming week you will pray about.
- A concrete kindness you can offer your partner this week.

PRAYER

Lord of life, help us to love from a foundation of peace rather than frenzy. Quiet our souls in your presence so that we may seek to be loving persons rather than striving to do that which only appears loving. Lift us from the tyranny of sloppy agape and help us to love with genuine hearts. Amen.

Real-Life Soul Mates

When Art and I got married, unmet and unvoiced expectations were a huge point of contention for us. I was desperate to figure out how to do this "wife" thing well. So I made note of what a "good wife" does.

- She cooks meatloaf.
- She vacuums every day so there are lines in the carpet indicating its cleanliness.
- She sticks love notes in his briefcase.
- She likes wearing lingerie and wears it three times a week.
- She hangs up the phone when he walks in the door.
- She learns facts about football and watches games with him.
- She prays for him every day.

And the list grew and grew.

Eventually, the list in my head of what a good wife does so completely overwhelmed me that I cried. I felt inadequate. I started to shut down. I assumed the list in my head was in Art's head too.

I grew bitter. And in a moment of complete exhaustion, I yelled, "Your expectations are ridiculous!" To which he replied, "What expectations?"

"The list . . . the list of hundreds of things I need to do to be a good wife," I sobbed.

His blank stare dumbfounded me. He had no such list.

I had so broadened my scope of things to do that I had diminished my ability to simply love him. Do less. Be more.

"Honey," I said feeling the entanglements of expectations loosening their grip on me, "I can't do everything good wives seem to do. But I can do three things. So tell me your top three things and I will do those well."

After all, I could spend a whole marriage doing a hundred things halfway with a bitter attitude and an overwhelmed spirit. Or I could do three things wholeheartedly with a smile on my face and love in my heart.

Art's three things were simple . . . be an emotionally and spiritually invested mom with our kids, take good care of my body and soul, and keep the house tidy. That's it.

He invited me to share my three things as well. They were for him to encourage me, be a strong spiritual leader for our family, and intentionally spend time with our kids.

Of course, we have other expectations in our marriage. But having a starting place of our top three expectations set us on a pattern of understanding how to realistically and creatively meet those expectations.

We had this first groundbreaking conversation twenty years ago. But to this day, we still narrow our scope to these three things, and it's helped us broaden our vision for a great marriage!

Art and Lysa TerKeurst

IT'S MY MARRIAGE AND I'LL CRY IF I WANT TO

"Don't cry!"

"It's okay to cry," Leslie whimpered.

We were having lunch at a favorite restaurant, talking about I don't know what when out of nowhere, or so it seemed, Leslie's eyes flooded with tears. Only moments before they were sparkling. "I know it's okay to cry," I confessed, "but can't you wait until we get in the car?"

My simple request only exacerbated the emotion I was trying to stifle. Leslie dabbed her eyes with a napkin, trying to retain her mascara, but the floodgates soon opened and the tears flowed like a stream.

I can't tell you how many times we have lived through similar scenes and neither of us could tell you what the issues were, but we can assure you that tears are a part of every marriage relationship. And it's a good thing. Research on crying has shown that tears contain chemicals related to stress. When people cry they are actually washing away the harmful effects of stress. William Frey, in his book *Crying: The Mystery of Tears*, suggests that women, whom society allows to cry more openly and frequently, are able to excrete their "stress waste" more readily than men, who are conditioned to block this natural cleansing system.

Whatever the scientists have discovered about crying, God understood in the beginning. Did you know that God keeps a record of your tears? The psalmist says they are listed on a scroll (see Ps. 56:8). God values our tears. Consider who God chose to be his spokesperson at the most critical time in Israel's history—Jeremiah, "the weeping prophet"! Jeremiah didn't always have the words to describe his feelings, but his tears often served as his message. He was not ashamed to bury his head in his hands and sob aloud. He was not ashamed to cry.

How about you? When your words fail, can you let the tears flow? Can you identify with the woman in the opening chapter of Lamentations: "Bitterly she weeps at night, tears are on her cheeks" (1:2)? Can you identify with the prophet who said, "Streams of tears flow from my eyes because my people are destroyed. My eyes will flow unceasingly, without relief, until the LORD looks down from heaven and sees" (Lam. 3:48–51)? How about with Jesus as he wept at the death of his friend Lazarus (John 11:35)?

Let me be honest. I'm not totally comfortable with tears. When Leslie cries I still cringe. But I have learned that tears, hers and mine, are essential to a growing marriage. And I have learned to value the tears of my wife—just as God does.

Part of becoming soul mates is learning that there is no shame in tears. Sure, crying in the middle of a restaurant is nobody's idea of a good time, but if onlookers don't understand the tenderness of tears between a married couple, that's their problem!

FROM GOD'S WORD

And he who sits on the throne will shelter them with his presence. 'Never again will they hunger, never again will they thirst. The sun will not beat down on them,' nor any scorching heat. For the Lamb at the center of the throne will be their shepherd; 'he will lead them to springs of living water.' 'And God will wipe away every tear from their eyes.'

Revelation 7:15–17

YOUR TURN

- How have tears played a part in your marriage? How would each of you rate on a "tearfulness scale"?
- Give an example of a time you personally cried with your spouse. How comfortable was that experience for you?
- How does Christ's response to the death of Lazarus impact you? What does it tell you about expressing your feelings through tears?
- Discuss how your spiritual well-being may be linked to your emotional well-being in marriage.
- How can each of you more effectively take into account the emotional well-being of your partner? How can you give him or her the freedom to express even sad emotions?

SOUL TO SOUL

To deepen your spiritual intimacy this next week, make note of:

- What you gained from this session together.
- A pressure point in your partner's upcoming week you will pray about.
- A concrete kindness you can offer your partner this week.

PRAYER

God of compassion, you who have known true joy and experienced true sorrow, help us to understand our emotions deeply. Enable us to draw on the gift of tears as a source of strength for our marriage. Let us learn, even this week, to be comfortable with tears in our marriage. Amen.

Real-Life Soul Mates

We cringe when we're at a wedding and the groom makes the iconic promise to his new wife: "I promise to make you happy." Usually everybody at the wedding smiles. Maybe you hear an "aw." It sounds so romantic and innocuous, but honestly, it's a setup for disillusionment. Or worse.

We fight the urge to stand up and scream at the couple, "You can't keep that promise! Nobody can!" (Don't worry, we don't.)

As sweet as it sounds, we can't find ultimate happiness in marriage—no matter how fantastic our marriage is. We need a wider vision of life in community. When I (John Mark) officiate a wedding, I usually quote from Genesis 2, where God said, "It's not good for the man to be alone." I make the point that we were created for relationship. Designed by the Creator himself to live in community. And then I apply that idea to marriage.

But over the years we've learned to carry that idea one step further. Adam and Eve were never supposed to stay Adam and Eve. They were supposed to "be fruitful and increase in number." To become a family, then a tribe, then a nation, then a thriving global civilization.

This has stunning implications for how we do marriage and spirituality. And it stands in stark opposition to our culture. The dangerous cocktail of American hyper-individualism and Hollywood's romanticism puts a soul-crushing weight on every marriage. Without meaning to, we often deposit all our deep, innate desires for meaning, purpose, and satisfaction onto our spouse's shoulders. We expect them to fulfill us relationally, emotionally, sexually, and even spiritually. In our romantic quest to make each other happy, we often end up suffocating the person we most love.

We've learned that both marriage and spirituality need to be done in community. For years Tammy and I lived in isolation. I was an overbusy pastor and an introvert. We kept our private life, well, private. But after almost a decade of marriage, we realized we needed to live in community. So we invited another couple we knew to move into a house on our street. We started doing life *together*. Then we grabbed a few other families, including a single dad with six kids at home. Then Tammy's best friend moved into the neighborhood to join us. We ended up becoming a *family*. We eat, drink, play, vacation, pray, worship, cry, celebrate, and just live life *together*.

For us, it's changed everything. Tammy, who is more extroverted, gets a huge chunk of her relational needs met from the other women in our community. I get a regular kick in the pants to love her well. The suffocating pressure to fulfill each other is spread out over our community, and ultimately, onto God himself.

There's no doubt that life is harder in community. But it's also better. *Way* better. And now that we've discovered this new way of life, we're never going back.

John Mark and Tammy Comer

RAPUNZEL'S LOVE LESSON

The fairy tale *Rapunzel* is the story of a beautiful young girl imprisoned in a tower with an old witch who insistently tells her she is ugly. One day when Rapunzel gazes from the window in her tower, she sees her Prince Charming standing below. He is enchanted by her beauty and tells her to let her long, golden tresses down from the window. The prince then braids her hair into a ladder and climbs up to rescue her.

The implicit message of this fairy tale is simple but profound. Rapunzel's prison is really not the tower but her fear that she is ugly and unlovable. The mirroring eyes of her prince, however, tell her that she is loved, and thus she is set free from the tyranny of her own imagined worthlessness.

In a sense we are all like Rapunzel, enslaved by the fear of rejection, yearning to be valued by a prince or princess. But in our counseling office we have seen enough couples to know that some spouses are especially troubled by the fear of being unlovable. They are afraid that they are not loved because they feel unlovable. Susan, married just under a year, came to us with her husband, Don, because she repeatedly questioned her worth. "Sometimes I just don't know how Don can love me," she would say. "I feel so guilty; like I don't deserve to have such a good husband."

Jonah would have understood Susan's feelings of inadequacy.

When God called Jonah to preach to the city of Nineveh, Jonah ran away. And when a storm threatened to capsize the boat he was on, Jonah knew immediately whose fault the storm was. "Throw me into the sea," he said, "and it will become calm" (1:12). Only when he was trapped in the belly of the great fish did Jonah stop running and face up to God.

Sometimes love is a difficult gift to grasp. The grace of being loved and accepted unconditionally is incomprehensible. And though our partner will certainly fall short of this kind of perfect love, we must still come to accept the gracious gift of God's eternal love: "For God so loved the world that he gave his one and only Son, that whoever believes in him shall not perish but have eternal life" (John 3:16).

Like Rapunzel or like Susan, some of us fear that we are not lovable, that even a prince or princess cannot change that. And some of us, like Jonah, cannot fathom why God would choose to love us. That is why John reminds us: "As the Father has loved me, so have I loved you. Now remain in my love" (John 15:9).

FROM GOD'S WORD

Therefore, there is now no condemnation for those who are in Christ Jesus, because through Christ Jesus the law of the Spirit who gives life has set you free from the law of sin and death. For what the law was powerless to do because it was weakened by the flesh, God did by sending his own Son in the likeness of sinful flesh to be a sin offering. And so he condemned sin in the flesh, in order that the righteous requirement of the law might be fully met in us, who do not live according to the flesh but according to the Spirit.

ROMANS 8:1–4

YOUR TURN

- Why do you think it is difficult to accept God's gracious unconditional love?
- Give an example of how your personal significance was recently affirmed by your partner.
- Have you been trapped in the prison of fear of rejection?
- What is one thing your partner can do to affirm your worth and value?
- Discuss ways you can work as a couple to strengthen your awareness of God's love and grace this week.

SOUL TO SOUL

To deepen your spiritual intimacy this next week, make note of:

- What you gained from this session together.
- A pressure point in your partner's upcoming week you will pray about.
- A concrete kindness you can offer your partner this week.

PRAYER

Gracious God, grant us this week the power to live in full knowledge of your unconditional love. And help us to give the same unconditional love to each other. At times it is tough, so we ask you to keep us motivated. Thank you for your love to us. Amen.

Real-Life Soul Mates

Over the years, my wife, Cindy, and I have taken specific passages that we have studied in God's Word and used them as a "personalized prayer guide" for each other. For example, take Psalm 15. That's a wonderful psalm where David lists ten traits that should be reflected in each Christian's life, then caps them off with a promise, "He who does these things will never be shaken."

With all the ups and downs of living in a stressful world, an "unshakable life" is certainly something we both want to have! So we've taken the ten traits listed there and specifically prayed that they will be daily reflected in our loved one's life.

For example, "He who walks with integrity, works righteousness and speaks truth in his heart," becomes a personalized prayer for my wife: "Lord, keep Cindy walking in integrity; may she choose to do the right thing today, even in those times when it's difficult; and may your Word so fill her heart that her words to herself and to others echo your truth." Or, to apply another verse of Psalm 15 ("He swears to his own hurt and does not change"), she would pray for me, "Lord, may John be a man who always keeps his promises. Even if it's costly. Lord, may he always put commitment ahead of convenience."

Studying a passage together, then praying that God's truth will deeply reside in each other's life is a great way to build spiritual bonds!

John and Cindy Trent

Session Fourteen

LISTENING WITH THE THIRD EAR

"The road to the heart," wrote Voltaire, "is the ear." So true. Carefully listening to your partner is the quickest path to intimacy. The problem is that most of us confuse hearing with listening. There is a simple skill, however, that can immediately help most couples improve their ability to really listen. It is called reflection.

Like a mirror reflecting an image, good listeners reflect the emotions of the people they are with. Here are some examples:

Husband: I don't care what my boss says, I'm not giving up those vacation days.
Wife: You sound pretty resolved.

Wife: I can't believe they canceled the party. I was so excited for this thing.
Husband: You sound really disappointed.

Listening to what your partner is feeling is far more important than hearing what they are saying. Theodor Reik calls it listening with "the third ear." It allows you to tap into the emotional message that underlies nearly every verbal message. And when you can do this for each other, you immediately strengthen your bond as soul mates.

By the way, reflective listening is the best way we know of to defuse a potential conflict. If your partner starts hurling "you" statements such as "You are always late," try not to become defensive by saying, "I am not." Instead, reflect the emotional message by saying, "I know it upsets you when I'm late. It's got to be exasperating." The point is to listen for the message underlying the actual words. "You are always late" means "I'm upset."

Jesus understood this. When he encountered the emotionally disturbed demonic man who lived among the tombs in Gadara, the man was shouting at Jesus: "What do you want with us, Son of God? Have you come here to torture us?" (Matt. 8:29). Jesus could have turned and walked away. He certainly didn't deserve to be talked to like that. Jesus would have been justified in leaving the poor man to his own devices. But instead, Jesus listened with the third ear. He not only heard the words that the man shouted, but he listened for the message of the emotions behind the words. Jesus understood that the man's outburst was really a cry for help.

Since most people talk at the rate of 120 words per minute, and since most spoken material can be comprehended equally well at rates up to 250 words per minute, plenty of extra time is available for mental activity during a typical conversation. So instead of using that time to think of what you want to say next, use it to tap into the emotions of your partner. Use it to listen with the third ear.

FROM GOD'S WORD

Do not let any unwholesome talk come out of your mouths, but only what is helpful for building others up according to their needs, that it may benefit those who listen.

EPHESIANS 4:29

YOUR TURN

- How do each of you practice the art of reflective listening? What do you consciously do to make it work?
- Give an example of how you personally have practiced the art of listening with your partner. What made it difficult or easy?
- Does reflective listening come more easily to one of you than it does to the other? Why or why not?
- How does listening relate to your spiritual journey?
- What is one way you can each practice reflective listening to strengthen the bonds of your marriage this week?

SOUL TO SOUL

To deepen your spiritual intimacy this next week, make note of:

- What you gained from this session together.
- A pressure point in your partner's upcoming week you will pray about.
- A concrete kindness you can offer your partner this week.

PRAYER

Gracious God, you who listen to the messages often buried beneath the words in our prayers, create in us the capacity to listen to each other as you listen to us. Through the inspiration of your Holy Spirit, enlighten, instruct, and guide us in the art of listening this week. Amen.

Real-Life Soul Mates

Everyone's marriage is different when it comes to spiritual intimacy. Some people are very dedicated to making sure they pray and read the Bible together on a daily basis. In our case, we have been married for decades, and during this time, we have never found "the secret" to having daily quiet times together, regular times of prayer, and so on. Part of that is the way we are wired. One of us is a reader who likes quiet, alone times with the Lord. One is a verbal processor who would prefer that the two of us spend more time together processing what God is teaching us. But, despite our differences, we still feel very connected spiritually.

How is that?

We stay connected by talking often. We can wake up in the middle of the night and talk. We have coffee together every morning and talk. We talk on the phone often whether we're in the same town or miles apart. We know each other's hearts.

And knowing each other's hearts, we pray for each other as we go through the day.

We pray short prayers together when a subject arises. We give thanks to God when we both appreciate a person, a place, or an event. We use intercessory prayers when we encounter a traffic accident, for instance, or are touched by something we've seen in the media or heard on the phone. We pray when one of our kids is facing a key decision or a tough situation. We pray when others call us and ask for prayer. We pray together at meals. But we don't begin each day in prayer or end it at night with prayer. Why? We have different schedules, one of us is often on the road, and we have different sleep patterns.

We minister together. When we were at University Presbyterian Church in Seattle doing college ministry at the University of Washington, we shared the position. We were both the "college directors." The split wasn't because we had small kids at home, but because we were united by a call and by our passion for university students to meet Christ and grow in their faith. We had intern meetings in our home; we hosted events together; we were a team. When we were chosen to lead Young Life, we came together. One of us has the title of president, but both of us feel called and committed to what we're doing.

On a somewhat regular basis around our coffee in the morning, we read *Jesus Calling* and pray.

When one of us has a speaking or writing responsibility, we provide some "editing assistance" but only if asked.

We cheer each other on.

Maybe someday we will be more regular in our approach, but for now, it seems to be working, and we're excited to be sharing our lives together.

Denny and Marilyn Rydberg

Session Fifteen

IS PRAYER YOUR STEERING WHEEL OR YOUR SPARE TIRE?

Praying together is not easy for us. Oh, we pray as a couple before meals, and we pray together when there is a special need or crisis, but we aren't the kind of couple who kneels beside our bed each night. We might be better persons if we did, but we don't. I suppose we could blame our busy and fickle schedules, but the truth is we just haven't made the effort to build a consistent shared prayer time into our lives.

We admire couples who do and we covet the rewards they surely reap. For as Jesus has said, "If two of you on earth agree about anything they ask for, it will be done for them by my Father in heaven. For where two or three gather in my name, there am I with them" (Matt. 18:19–20).

Still, one thing we do every day is pray for each other. Whether together or in separate cities, we remember each other in our daily prayers. We made that commitment on our wedding day, and Leslie had the reference of Philippians 1:3–11 engraved inside my wedding band. It's a prayer that says, "I thank my God every time I remember you. . . . I always pray with joy because of your partnership in the gospel from the first day until now."

Sometimes one of us will say to the other, "I'll be praying for you today," but most of the time there is just a quiet assurance that our partner is lifting us up with prayers.

"Prayer—secret, fervent, believing prayer—lies at the root of all personal godliness," wrote William Carey. Prayer transports us into the deepest levels of the human spirit. It is in prayer that we begin to think God's thoughts and desire the things he desires (see Rom. 8:26–27). And we believe that praying for each other is critically important to guiding soul mates. Corrie ten Boom asks a poignant question about prayer that every couple should answer: "Is prayer your steering wheel or your spare tire?"

The great giants of the faith viewed prayer as the main source of direction in their lives. Martin Luther declared, "I have so much business I cannot get on without spending three hours daily in prayer." John Wesley said, "God does nothing but in answer to prayer," and he backed up his conviction by devoting two hours daily to praying. The words of Mark, "Very early in the morning, while it was still dark, Jesus got up, left the house and went off to a solitary place, where he prayed," stand as a commentary on the lifestyle of Jesus (1:35).

Fortunately, you don't have to be a "giant in the faith" to pray daily. In fact, you may just be learning to pray (even the disciples, in Luke 11:1, implored Jesus, "Lord, teach us to pray"). But as long as you are spending time in prayer, you can be assured that God will make himself present in your life and in your marriage.

FROM GOD'S WORD

When you pray, do not be like the hypocrites, for they love to pray standing in the synagogues and on the street corners to be seen by others. Truly I tell you, they have received their reward in full.

But when you pray, go into your room, close the door and pray to your Father, who is unseen. Then your Father, who sees what is done in secret, will reward you. And when you pray, do not keep on babbling like pagans, for they think they will be heard because of their many words. Do not be like them, for your Father knows what you need before you ask him.

MATTHEW 6:5–8

YOUR TURN

- Why do you think Jesus preached against hypocrites who love to pray in public? Why did he preach against "babbling" pray-ers?
- What were your experiences of prayer in your family growing up?
- Give an example of a time when you offered intercessory prayer for your partner. How did it impact your role in the situation at hand?
- Talk with your partner about the times you spend in personal prayer. Discuss how often you pray for each other.
- What can you do, in practical terms, to keep from treating prayer as a spare tire—only for emergencies?

SOUL TO SOUL

To deepen your spiritual intimacy this next week, make note of:

- What you gained from this session together.
- A pressure point in your partner's upcoming week you will pray about.
- A concrete kindness you can offer your partner this week.

PRAYER

Gracious God, teach us to pray with meaning. Save us from the torrent of words which may be our cover-up for reality. Let us be authentic with our prayers and remind us this week to be grateful for every good quality we see in each other. Help us to surround our soul mate in prayer and sustain our marriage covenant through your grace. Amen.

Real-Life Soul Mates

Five o'clock this morning I was wide awake. Something troubling was on my mind.

Jill stirred slightly. "Are you awake?" I whispered.

"Oh yes," she replied, "About a couple of hours ago."

"Are you thinking about it?" I asked.

"Of course," she replied, "can't get it out of my mind."

"Do you want to talk about it?" I ventured.

"What is there new to say?" she responded.

"So let's pray about it," I suggested.

But what to pray? What could we say that we hadn't said before?

"You go first," I said.

"No, you," she countered, "Okay?"

Where to begin? My acrostic that I'd taught a hundred times—Praise, Repent, Ask, Yourself—didn't seem right.

Too stiff. Praying wouldn't come. I felt as cold as the Wisconsin February morning outside the window. So I just started to tell the Lord what was going on inside me. As I did so, Jill's hand searched for mine and held it tight. Her grip said, "That's what I think, that's how I feel. Go on, go on." The words began to form, the feelings began to flow, the petitions and longings became apparent. I stopped and she carried right on without a break. Adding to what I had said, remembering what I had omitted, repeating those words which framed her thoughts, and articulating my words with her own.

Two hearts beating as one. Two prayers, one Lord, one faith, one burden, one hope.

Praying together binds on earth two people whose hearts are bound to the One in heaven. It is one of marriage's deepest joys and greatest blessings.

Stuart and Jill Briscoe

THE DEADLY EMOTION OF ANGER

It would be tough to find another emotion that has caused married couples more difficulty than anger. Why do we get angry at the person we love the most? Why do we allow ourselves to get angry when we know in advance that we will need to apologize? Why do we raise our voices when it does no good?

We have seen firsthand in our marriage counseling how different people use different means for dealing with their anger. Some try to deny it by calling it something else. They confuse anger with fatigue, nervousness, or being uptight. Others try to deal with their anger by suppressing it. They make every effort to keep it from showing (this usually leads to a phony, emotional, saccharine sweetness). Still others try to spiritualize their anger by talking about anger that is righteous and anger that is unrighteous (which usually means "my anger is righteous and yours is the other kind"). We have even seen some couples where one partner flaunts anger: "This is the way God made me. You know what I am like, so you just might as well get used to it. It's in my genes."

Well, anger is not inherited. How we express our anger is learned and can be unlearned. Whether suppressed, spiritualized, or flaunted, anger will do its destructive deeds to even the best of marriages—unless we first of all understand what it is.

Anger begins as a physiological response to a real or imagined threat. The involuntary nervous system goes to work whenever the brain signals that injury is a possibility. First, sweat breaks out in the palms of our hands. Then the heart begins to pound twice as hard as usual. The throat gets dry. The pituitary gland pours adrenaline into the bloodstream, and suddenly the body is ready for battle.

Any attempt to spiritualize this involuntary response is futile. It is neither moral nor immoral. It is simply the body's response as God made us. But out of this response can come terrible behavior. This is why Paul wrote to the Ephesians, "In your anger do not sin: Do not let the sun go down while you are still angry" (4:26).

You see, it is not whether you get angry or not, but what you do with your anger once it kicks in. Paul encourages us to "be careful to do what is right . . . [and] live at peace with everyone" (Rom. 12:17–18). He warns us, "Do not take revenge" (Rom. 12:19).

FROM GOD'S WORD

Do not repay anyone evil for evil. Be careful to do what is right in the eyes of everyone. If it is possible, as far as it depends on you, live at peace with everyone. Do not take revenge, my dear friends, but leave room for God's wrath, for it is written: "It is mine to avenge; I will repay," says the Lord. On the contrary: "If your enemy is hungry, feed him; if he is thirsty, give him something to drink. In doing this, you will heap burning coals on his head." Do not be overcome by evil, but overcome evil with good.

ROMANS 12:17–21

YOUR TURN

- What is the difference between feeling angry and committing a sin? Some believe they are the same thing. What about you?
- Give an example of a time when your partner's response enabled you to transform your anger into a positive outcome. What can both of you learn from that?
- Have you ever confused fatigue, nervousness, or being uptight with anger? How can you avoid this common error?
- What can you do, in practical terms, to resolve anger before it erupts? What can you do, for example, before discussing a typically hot issue?
- Since anger is inevitable, how can you and your partner work together to anticipate it and deal with it constructively?

SOUL TO SOUL

To deepen your spiritual intimacy this next week, make note of:

- What you gained from this session together.
- A pressure point in your partner's upcoming week you will pray about.
- A concrete kindness you can offer your partner this week.

PRAYER

Our Father in heaven, you who are slow to anger and quick to show compassion, empower us to use our anger constructively. We accept anger as part of being human, but please save us from destructive anger or from the sin of using anger to manipulate each other. When we feel angry help us to call on you for guidance. Amen.

Real-Life Soul Mates

At the beginning of our marriage, Michael and I made a deliberate decision to invite God into our bedroom. That means we never go to bed angry.

We are committed to talking through our issues and getting full resolution before we go to sleep. The longest we've stayed up working through our stuff is 3:30 in the morning, but we will stay up longer if the situation calls for it.

Here are some of the prearranged agreements we have to make this work:

1. We don't bail out of the conversation and falsely apologize just to go to sleep.
2. We each need to have peace in our soul before we can call it done. Even on the rare occasion that we have a disagreement while Michael is traveling, all these agreements still apply and we follow this process over the phone.
3. We remain committed to respecting one another throughout the argument.
4. When things get really tough, we have established that either one of us can initiate worship in the midst of our argument. Not that either of us feels like it at that time or that it's easy, but if one of us says, "I think we should worship," the other would be hard pressed to say, "No."

Am I really going to tell God that I am too angry with my husband to acknowledge his goodness? No. This act breaks through any wall that we've hit; it causes the enemy to flee; it helps us to redirect our solutions toward hearing from the Lord; and it softens our hearts to hear one another again.

Taking these steps ensures that God's presence is welcome in our bedroom, which elevates the joy and intimacy in our relationship, sex life, and prayer life in and out of the bedroom.

Michael Jr. and Ebony

Session Seventeen

THE EXTRA MILE IN MARRIAGE

One of the most shocking statements Jesus ever made holds enough power to revolutionize your marriage.

He said: "If someone forces you to go one mile, go with him two miles."

Have you learned to apply the extra-mile principle to your marriage? Every husband and every wife knows how to walk the first mile. After all, our relationships couldn't survive without it. The first mile is what we know we have to do. It is taking out the trash, preparing dinner, or balancing the checkbook because we said we would do it.

So what's the second mile? At the time Jesus made this statement, the Roman army had a pesky practice of forcing men and boys who were nearby to carry its soldiers' packs. Being more civilized than other armies, the Romans limited the task to one mile. And every boy under Roman rule knew exactly how far that was. In fact, a boy often drove a stake into the ground precisely one mile from his house as a marker. This way, when a soldier required the task, the boy would walk exactly a mile down the road to the stake, set the pack on the other side, and be done with it. That was all he was required to do and nobody expected more.

Jesus used this illustration to point out that we sometimes do the same thing in our relationships. We measure out exactly how much is expected and do just that, nothing more. Let's face it, with our hectic pace, most of us do just enough to squeak by even in the relationship that matters most. So, yes, we grumble and take out the trash or we whine and make the meal, but only because we have to. Jesus, however, says there is a better way—to do more than the minimum.

The extra mile turns the ordinary into the extraordinary, the expected into the unexpected. You walk the extra mile for your partner, for example, when you take out the trash with a smile or prepare a meal with a special touch. The extra mile turns responsibility into opportunity. When you are walking the extra mile in marriage, your attitude shifts from "have to" to "want to." That's why the apostle Peter said, "Offer hospitality to one another without grumbling" (1 Peter 4:9).

Common courtesy is an example of the extra mile in some marriages. It sounds funny, but courtesy isn't so common after even a short period of marriage. We take "thank you" and "you're welcome" for granted. We forget to say "please" at the table. The apostle Paul understood the importance of this principle in our relationships. He urges us to be kind and loving toward one another (Gal. 5:22).

So practice the extra mile in your marriage. It is more powerful than dynamite. Try it.

FROM GOD'S WORD

And if anyone wants to sue you and take your shirt, hand over your coat as well. If anyone forces you to go one mile, go with them two miles. Give to the one who asks you, and do not turn away from the one who wants to borrow from you.

MATTHEW 5:40–42

YOUR TURN

- Why do you think Christ was so shocking in his definition of love? Do you believe it is obtainable?
- How have you struggled with the extra-mile principle? Have weariness or busyness been obstacles for you? What else makes the extra mile in marriage difficult for you?
- What price do most couples pay for doing only the bare minimum, only what is expected in marriage?
- Give an example of a time when you benefited from the extraordinary love of your partner.
- How can you work together to practice the extra-mile principle in your marriage? Give some examples of ways you might walk the extra mile for one another.

SOUL TO SOUL

To deepen your spiritual intimacy this next week, make note of:

- What you gained from this session together.
- A pressure point in your partner's upcoming week you will pray about.
- A concrete kindness you can offer your partner this week.

PRAYER

Gracious God, teach us to love each other as you love us. Teach us to walk the extra mile in patience, forgiveness, and kindness when we may be tempted this week to get by with the bare minimum. Give us the quality of gratitude that spills over to moments of courtesy and unexpected love in our marriage. In the name of Christ, amen.

Real-Life Soul Mates

Spiritual intimacy really came to life for my wife and me when I committed my life to Christ on July 4, 1972. I immediately knew that I had a lot of catching up to do. But with my new spiritual commitment, my wife's spiritual growth also increased and our relationship improved immeasurably.

Four practices have been especially significant in our spiritual growth. First, we attended a Christian Marriage Encounter weekend and learned how to express our love for each other better. Second, we read the *One-Year Bible* together. Even though my travels took me out of town a great deal, I called her each evening at an appointed time and we discussed what the day's Scriptures had meant to each of us. Third, every day we each try to do something for the other that the other is completely capable of doing for him- or herself. For instance, my wife has not opened her car door a half-dozen times since I became a Christian. Each time I walk around the car I'm reminded that here is the most important person on Earth to me. Alternately, when I arise in the morning she will ask me if I'm ready for my tea or coffee and I'll say, "Yes, but I'll get it." Her response is, "No, let me do it." Fourth, we hug fifteen to thirty times each day. These are neither long nor sensual, but they communicate our love in a significant manner.

These steps are simple, but they have advanced our spiritual walk and developed our love for one another.

Zig and Jean Ziglar

HELP FOR THE ROMANTICALLY IMPAIRED

It was our one-year anniversary—June 30, 1985. Whew! A whole year of being married. And now the celebration. Just how would we commemorate this important milestone? A romantic dinner and a walk under the stars? A rosy bouquet or a box of Godiva chocolates? Nope. We packed a picnic lunch with tuna fish sandwiches and Diet Pepsi and drove from Pasadena up the coast to Santa Barbara, three or so hours away. It was Les's idea. *Okay*, I thought, *this could be fun*. We'll have time to talk as we drive and we can eat our lunch on the beach. But Les, now in graduate school, had a different idea. He was one week into a stressful summer school course, taking Greek! So he brought along a taped lecture to listen to on our drive and a pack of flash cards to study for his next exam.

So much for romance, at least on that day. I shouldn't paint an incorrect picture; Les can be very romantic. On my birthday this year, for example, he took me to the swankiest restaurant in town and had prearranged with the maitre d' to have a gift delivered to our table with my favorite dessert.

Still, in our home, romance can be a hit-or-miss endeavor. Of course, I do my part. Like the time I planned a weekend getaway as a surprise for Les. That's when I learned he doesn't think surprises are very romantic! Or the time I thought he would enjoy going to a theater production instead of skiing with his friends. He didn't.

Well, if you don't already know, we haven't discovered *the* secret to romance in marriage. Maybe that makes us romantically impaired. But we have discovered that a big part of cultivating romance is learning to accept and respect each other's differences. Why? Because what is romantic to one person is not necessarily enjoyable to the other. For example, if Les has an unfinished task hanging over his head, I know to wait till he is done. Then he is fully present and ready to go out on the town. On the other hand, when I have a looming deadline hanging over my head, Les knows I love to be surprised with a diversion.

So Les is a little more practical, and I'm a little more frivolous. Does this affect our ability to cultivate romance? You bet. But what about you? What differences might impede your romantic endeavors? Can you accept and respect those differences? When Paul wrote to the Romans he said, "Accept one another, then, just as Christ accepted you, in order to bring praise to God" (15:7). I don't know if romance is what Paul had in mind with that advice, but it certainly applies.

FROM GOD'S WORD

Above all, love each other deeply, because love covers over a multitude of sins. Offer hospitality to one another without grumbling. Each of you should use whatever gift you have received to serve others, as faithful stewards of God's grace in its various forms.

1 Peter 4:8–10

YOUR TURN

- Scripture says that "love covers a multitude of sins." What does this mean to you, and how does it apply to marriage?
- Give an example of a time when you tried to be romantic with your partner and it didn't turn out that way. Are you able to laugh about it?
- How is your partner's idea of romance different from yours? Discuss your idea of the perfectly romantic day or evening.
- In what specific ways do you appreciate your partner's "romance language"—even when it is different from your own?
- The romance that couples enjoy decades after their wedding is often the result of how they built romance into their early years together. What are you doing to make romance a natural part of your marriage?

SOUL TO SOUL

To deepen your spiritual intimacy this next week, make note of:

- What you gained from this session together.
- A pressure point in your partner's upcoming week you will pray about.
- A concrete kindness you can offer your partner this week.

PRAYER

Our Father, we thank you for creating in us the joy of romantic love. Grant us the ability to spark the heart of each other by responding to the need for tenderness. Help us receive with joy the gift of romantic love from our partner. Amen.

Real-Life Soul Mates

Last night the temperature plummeted close to zero degrees Fahrenheit. Since we normally heat the house with our woodstove, the bedroom was cold when we climbed into bed. Fortunately, that only made us more eager to snuggle closely together in each other's arms for our regular bedtime prayers under the covers.

For many years we have enjoyed starting and ending most days by praying together in each other's arms. We pray about the day's special worries and pressing problems, and often the prayer gets interrupted while we share a joy or sorrow we had forgotten to mention over dinner or dishes. Together we lift each other's biggest burdens to the Lord. And there's always time to ask God to watch over our children.

Devotional snuggling also helps us get over angry quarrels. You cannot hold on to your resentment if you honestly start to open your heart to the heavenly Father.

Those few minutes of warmth and closeness with each other and with openness and petition to God have become regular moments of quiet joy and tenderness. And just a little more time for prayer is an unbeatable excuse to delay jumping out of bed on a sleepy morning.

We would be the first to confess that the warm feelings we experience in our devotional snuggling are not limited to the pleasure that flows from prayer. We are also certain that the God who inspired the Song of Songs does not mind at all. After all, both physical and spiritual intimacy were his idea.

Ronald and Arbutus Sider

Session Nineteen

OUR LONGING FOR BELONGING

Several weeks ago a number of couples from our church were gathered around a long restaurant table on a Sunday evening. We were in one of those peculiar seating arrangements where the wives were at one end of the table and the husbands at the other. When we began placing our orders with the server, the first person in a couple, for the sake of the bill, would say, "I belong to him," or "He belongs to me." No one around this table of fellowshipping couples was a loner. Everyone belonged to someone else.

It is wonderful to belong. Belongingness is an awareness of being wanted and accepted, of being cared for and enjoyed. It is the "we" feeling experienced when we know our partner appreciates us and wants to be with us. Belonging, however, doesn't begin in marriage. We begin the quest for belonging as soon as we enter the world. As infants and children we must be nurtured into a sense of belongingness with our family. In the turbulent teen years we try desperately to belong, to be with the "in" crowd. And certainly as young adults we long to belong.

But something wonderful happens in the quest for belongingness when we get married. By joining with another person for life, belongingness has an altogether new opportunity to flourish.

A healthy marriage cannot survive without a sense of belonging. While marriage can survive great inconvenience, job loss, and physical illness, it can never survive rejection and aloneness. A married couple may have all the material things they can possibly need, but if they do not have a sense of belonging together they will starve emotionally. As Victor Hugo put it, "The supreme happiness of life is in the conviction that we are loved."

How are feelings of belongingness generated? By doing things together, by sharing common concerns, by trusting each other with responsibilities, by praying for each other, by laughing at things nobody else finds funny, by knowing what your partner is really thinking in a social setting, by sharing a meaningful insight, by doing nothing together. The list for cultivating belongingness could literally go on and on. Every couple has their own style of belonging.

And yet, our sense of belongingness, even in marriage, is nothing compared to the belonging we enjoy as Christians. God has called us by name and we are his. "Truly I tell you, anyone who gives you a cup of water in my name because *you belong to the Messiah* will certainly not lose their reward" (Mark 9:41, italics added). We belong to God, and he cares for us.

The ultimate source for generating belongingness in marriage is found in sharing a belonging to God.

FROM GOD'S WORD

Do not fear, for I have redeemed you; I have summoned you by name; you are mine. When you pass through the waters, I will be with you; and when you pass through the rivers, they will not sweep over you. When you walk through the fire, you will not be burned; the flames will not set you ablaze. For I am the LORD, your God, the Holy One of Israel, your Savior.

ISAIAH 43:1–3

YOUR TURN

- What do you think Christ means when he says he will make his home with us?
- Give an example of a time when you felt a keen sense of belonging with your partner. What made it so?
- When do you most often long to belong, and in what ways?
- How was belongingness cultivated in your family as you were growing up?
- What is one thing you would like your partner to do to make you feel more like you belong? What is one thing you can do to create the same sense for your partner?

SOUL TO SOUL

To deepen your spiritual intimacy this next week, make note of:

- What you gained from this session together.
- A pressure point in your partner's upcoming week you will pray about.
- A concrete kindness you can offer your partner this week.

PRAYER

Dear Lord, we bow our heads and our hearts in respect of your presence within our lives and especially in our home. Increase our sense of belonging to you and to each other this week. The more you dwell within our marriage, the stronger our partnership and the deeper our conviction of our love will be. Amen.

Real-Life Soul Mates

It might surprise you to know how we cultivate spiritual intimacy in our marriage. After all, we pastor a church—so you might predict that we'd tell you how we read the Bible, pray, and worship God together.

Okay. Sure. We do those things. And they're important to us. But we discovered something about spiritual intimacy—about walking together with God as a couple—as we celebrated our thirty-seventh wedding anniversary this year. We began reminiscing, talking about our adventures through the years.

Starting a church in 1980 and now leading three campuses was at the top of the list. Having three children at home and wrapping them in "swaddling clothes" was pretty awesome. Raising those three children who are all serving the Lord in significant ways and now beginning the grandparent adventure was up there too. Building church buildings and personal houses was quite a challenge. Hiking the Grand Canyon and many other peaks and lakes around the great Northwest also made our list. Learning to scuba dive together and riding our bikes over the Cascade Mountains several times have all been great challenges.

About then, as we were reviewing our married life together, we realized the secret to spiritual intimacy involves more than reading the Bible and shared prayers. It's staying engaged in this adventure called life together as we do our best to walk in the footsteps of Jesus—together. It's calling on God when facing cancer and hepatitis C—together. Riding or hiking all day—together. Working out the next season of church life—together. And figuring out what we're going to eat tonight—together.

The big deals and the little deals we keep working through together. It's not so much how you do it or what you do; it's doing it together. After all, you can read God's Word, go to church, and pray as a couple. But if you're not doing life together and inviting God to be part of that life in both big and little moments, you're bound to feel disconnected. You'll never enjoy true spiritual intimacy as a couple.

The Bible says no weapon formed against you will prevail (see Isa. 54:17), but anything that divides you can cause you to fall (see Mark 3:25). So we keep doing life together: a day with our granddaughter, a hike on Mount Rainier, a service at church, or a trip to preach somewhere in the world. Doing all those things together with God keeps spiritual intimacy alive and well in our marriage.

So do the adventures of life together. And oh, yes, keep having sex, too!

Casey and Wendy Treat

Session Twenty

THE CHURCH: A GREENHOUSE FOR GROWING SOUL MATES

A friend of ours told us a funny story about two guys who were fishing fanatics. On a recent Sunday morning they arose at 4 a.m. and drove more than a hundred miles into the mountains expecting to catch trout in a favorite, secluded stream whose location they had kept secret for years. After hiking two miles in from the road, their enthusiasm was dampened and the expedition aborted when they saw that rains farther upstream had produced silt, which muddied the waters and made fishing impractical. In their disgust one said to the other, "You might as well have stayed home and gone to church," to which his companion retorted with a straight face, "Oh, I can't go to church anyhow; my wife is sick."

How we choose to incorporate church into our marriage is critically important in becoming soul mates. Research has shown that couples who attend church, even once a month, increase their chances of staying married. Studies have also shown that churchgoers feel better about their marriages than those who don't worship together. Attending church provides couples with a shared sense of values and purpose in life. It also provides couples with a caring community of support.

To cultivate spiritual intimacy in your marriage without incorporating the church is like trying to drive a car without a steering wheel. Billy Graham says that "churchgoers are like coals in a fire. When they cling together, they keep the flame aglow; when they separate, they die out." Charles Colson, in his book *The Body*, says, "There is no such thing as Christianity apart from the Church." The church is more than a group of people who come together. It is a group of people who are called together by the gospel of Christ's love and forgiveness. As Paul puts it, the church is called into "fellowship with [God's] Son" (1 Cor. 1:9).

Paul also recognized the idea of the church as being God's family when he said we are "members of [God's] household" (Eph. 2:19). When Jesus taught his disciples to pray he did not say, "my Father"; he said, "our Father" (Matt. 6:9). We cannot live the Christian life in isolation. Membership in the church is not some optional extra. We cannot be fully Christian without belonging to and participating in the church. The New Testament makes it clear that to be a Christian is to be "in Christ." This means being a member of the new society of which Christ is the living head—the church.

From the beginning of our marriage, shared worship has been a systematic time of rest and renewal for our relationship. Dedicating a day of the week to attend church and worship with the body of Christ stabilizes our marriage and liberates us from the tyranny of productivity that fills our other days.

The church where we worship is a place of support and spiritual refueling. Singing hymns, learning from Scripture, worshiping God, and meeting with friends who share our spiritual quest is comforting and inspiring. Worshiping together buoys our relationship and makes the week ahead more meaningful.

FROM GOD'S WORD

Husbands, love your wives, just as Christ loved the church and gave himself up for her to make her holy, cleansing her by the washing with water through the word, and to present her to himself as a radiant church, without stain or wrinkle or any other blemish, but holy and blameless.

EPHESIANS 5:25–27

YOUR TURN

- Talk about the place worship holds for you as a couple. Rate its importance to you on a scale of one to ten.
- Give an example from your upbringing that illustrates the role worship has played in your life since you were a child.
- What are the goals you share as a couple for church involvement, and how are you working to meet them?
- What is the highlight of the typical worship service for you? If it is the music, what is your favorite chorus or hymn?
- How can the two of you work to make worship as a couple more meaningful to both of you?

SOUL TO SOUL

To deepen your spiritual intimacy this next week, make note of:

- What you gained from this session together.
- A pressure point in your partner's upcoming week you will pray about.
- A concrete kindness you can offer your partner this week.

PRAYER

Gracious God, grant us the strength, steadfastness, and faithfulness to live in harmony with your body, the church, in spite of its many human weaknesses. May our worship bring us renewal as it brings you joy, and may our fellowship be a witness of your love and our unity. In Christ's holy name we pray, amen.

Real-Life Soul Mates

Lots of people assume that since we work at a church, our spiritual life as a couple must be natural and easy. For us, that has not been the case. Spiritual intimacy is something we are always working toward.

One practice that has helped build our spiritual intimacy is our ongoing dedication to being part of a community group in our church. We were both living fully committed lives to Jesus when we were dating, but we really didn't know how to share the relationship we had with Jesus with each other.

Prayer with God on our own, individually, was natural. Prayer together wasn't. Worshiping God by myself was natural. Worship with Brandi wasn't.

Back then, and still to this day, we knew we needed help bringing the personal relationship we have with Jesus into our marriage relationship.

A few months before we married, we started our first community group at our first church plant in Kentucky. We wanted to start off our marriage surrounded by other couples who had similar Christian values. In that first community group we were the youngest couple by fifteen years. We were surrounded by couples who not only shared the same values, but who also had some marriage miles behind them. That first group was such a fun, engaging, learning time for each of us. We learned that everyone has struggles. What a relief.

Regardless of how perfect things might look on the outside, marriage is comprised of two imperfect people joining their shared histories to live the future out together.

But that group also taught us the power of sharing your story, the validation that can come from being vulnerable, and the accountability of confession.

After nineteen years of marriage we've been in many community groups over the years, and each one of them has helped us understand what it looks like to pursue Christ together. We've learned that having community within a small group of other couples is one of the best ways for us to spend time with God and cultivate spiritual intimacy together in our marriage.

Pete and Brandi Wilson

NAMES CAN NEVER HURT ME—OR CAN THEY?

Some years ago a team of psychologists did a study of a mill town in New England. Among other things, they were concerned with the criticism among the people who lived and worked so closely together. They found, first of all, that everyone in the community was guilty of criticizing everyone else. This was really no surprise. But they were really surprised to learn that all the community's members were absolutely scandalized whenever they heard that they themselves were the object of criticism. It was okay to criticize other people, but it was against the rules to be criticized.

Many sermons have been preached against criticism and its awful fruits. Many books have been written on the subject. But we are hard-pressed to find much of anything on how you are to respond in a marriage relationship when you inevitably become the object of your partner's criticism. It's an important issue. After all, you can do little to escape being criticized by the one who sees you up close, who knows how you live seven days a week. Being married is an act of opening yourself up to criticism. Sooner or later, whether he or she wants it to be critical or not, your partner will offhandedly critique something you do or even something you don't do.

In your contemplative moments you know that being criticized by your partner is part of "iron sharpening iron" (see Prov. 27:17), but that is little comfort when his or her iron seems to cut rather than polish. Being criticized by your spouse always hurts, probably because it contains a grain of truth. If your partner is like most people, he or she will pick some detail of your behavior and blow it all out of proportion. Even if you know it is simply an emotional exaggeration spurred on by a bad day at work, the truth buried in the criticism still stings.

No one was ever criticized more than Jesus. They called him a wine bibber, a glutton, one who enjoyed the fellowship of sinners more than the company of good people. He was accused of being a Samaritan, which was the same as being a traitor. Few have suffered more hostile scrutiny and unfair critique than Christ. The question is: How did he respond?

Jesus could have lashed out verbally against his accusers. He could have called down angels from heaven to take care of his critics. In one instance his disciples encouraged him to burn up the village where he was not welcome (Luke 9:51–55). But Jesus never struck back. What did he do? He forgave his critics. And ultimately, his response to criticism came on the cross when he prayed, "Father, forgive them, for they do not know what they are doing" (Luke 23:34).

FROM GOD'S WORD

Do not judge, and you will not be judged. Do not condemn, and you will not be condemned. Forgive, and you will be forgiven. . . . Why do you look at the speck of sawdust in your brother's eye and pay no attention to the plank in your own eye? How can you say to your brother, "Brother, let me take the speck out of your eye," when you yourself fail to see the plank in your own eye? You hypocrite, first take the plank out of your eye, and then you will see clearly to remove the speck from your brother's eye.

LUKE 6:37, 41–42

YOUR TURN

- Forgiveness is so fundamental to the message of Christ. What examples from Christ's life can you think of that illustrate this?
- Give an example of how you recently benefited from the ability of your partner to overlook a critical comment or behavior.
- When are you most likely to be critical of your partner?
- Have you talked about the difference between being criticized in public versus in private? What ground rules might help your relationship?
- How has your spouse's attentiveness and feedback contributed to your improvement? What works best for you in hearing critical information?

SOUL TO SOUL

To deepen your spiritual intimacy this next week, make note of:

- What you gained from this session together.
- A pressure point in your partner's upcoming week you will pray about.
- A concrete kindness you can offer your partner this week.

PRAYER

Gracious God, empower us with the capacity to forgive even when we have been undervalued or overcriticized by our partner. We offer this prayer in sincerity and in the name of Christ. Amen.

Real-Life Soul Mates

We were on our second date, in the lobby of the Disneyland Hotel waiting to get something to eat, and she had to use the restroom. When she came out, there were scores of people in the lobby, and I was in a goofy mood, so I said loudly enough for them all to hear, "Woman, I can't believe you kept me waiting for two hours."

Her immediate response was, "Well, I wouldn't have to if you didn't insist on having your mother live with us so I have to wait on her hand and foot every day." She yelled that, right across the lobby, on only our second date, and my first thought was, *I like this woman.*

I'm telling you this story because Nancy reminded me of it some time ago when things weren't going so well. She followed it with: "You know, when our marriage is at its best, you can listen and laugh and be spontaneous. You haven't been doing that for a while. I love that guy, and I miss that guy."

I knew what she was talking about.

"I miss that guy too," I told her. "I'd love to feel free like that. But I feel like I'm carrying so many burdens. I have personnel issues and financial challenges at work. I have writing projects and travel commitments. I feel like I'm carrying this weight all the time. I get what you're saying, but I need you to know, I'm doing the best I can."

"No, you're not," she responded immediately.

That was not the response I had anticipated. Everybody is supposed to nod their head sympathetically when you say, "I'm doing the best I can." But Nancy loves truth (and me) too much to do that. So she rang my bell. "No, you're not. You've talked about how it would be good to see a counselor, or an executive coach, or maybe a spiritual director. You've talked about building friendships, but I haven't seen you take steps toward any of that. No, you're not."

As soon as she said that, I knew she was right. I wasn't leaning into a God plan. I wasn't flourishing.

You see, God made you to flourish—to receive life from outside yourself, creating vitality within yourself, and producing blessing beyond yourself. Flourishing is God's gift and plan.

And helping each other live into God's gift and plan—as iron sharpens iron—is one of the ways we cultivate spiritual intimacy in our marriage.

John and Nancy Ortberg

LOVE MEANS HAVING TO EAT HUMBLE PIE

I did something dumb the other day. Leslie and I were driving in the bustling shopping section of downtown Seattle when I got an idea. "Hey, would you run in there and pick up a couple of those pens for me?" I asked Leslie. "I'll circle around the block and you can meet me on the corner." Leslie jumped out of the car and I began to circle.

Unfortunately, I was not very specific about which corner to meet her on. And then I discovered there were one-way streets I did not know about. The first thing I knew I had gone around many blocks and was trying desperately to get back on course. Finally I reached the corner where I thought Leslie would be. But she was on the other side of the street now, across two lanes of heavy traffic. I rolled down the window, honked the horn, and shouted, "Leslie, I'm over here!" She waved and made some motions I couldn't decipher. I waved back and ended up circling around four more blocks again to pick her up. You can guess what happened when she got into the car.

"What were you doing over there?" I snapped.

"What do you mean?" said Leslie. "You didn't tell me where to go, and I thought that was the corner you meant!"

We went around on this issue as much as I went around the city blocks. But once we both calmed down, I pulled the car over to the side and said those very difficult words that husbands have trouble saying: "I'm sorry."

I have a friend who has a saying I like. It always pops into my mind when I know I am wrong and should apologize. Here it is:

Humble pie is the only pastry that's never tasty.

Isn't that good? That goofy statement helps trigger my apology mechanism. After all, it's not easy to say "I'm sorry." Why? Because whenever we apologize we must first set aside our pride. Genuine sorrow is based on humility. There is no way around it. The writer of Proverbs understood this fact when he wrote: "When pride comes, then comes disgrace, but with humility comes wisdom" (11:2; see also 29:23).

I feel sorry for the person married to someone who never says, "I'm sorry." Without another piece of information about them, I can predict with confidence that their home is filled with conflict and quarrels. "Where there is strife, there is pride, but wisdom is found in those who take advice" (Prov. 13:10).

So remember, the next time you do something stupid, the next time you are in the wrong, 'fess up. Eat a little humble pie. It won't taste good, but it's the only sure way to say, "I'm sorry."

FROM GOD'S WORD

Do nothing out of selfish ambition or vain conceit. Rather, in humility value others above yourselves, not looking to your own interests but each of you to the interests of the others. In your relationships with one another, have the same mindset as Christ Jesus.

PHILIPPIANS 2:3–5

YOUR TURN

- The Bible underscores the importance of humility again and again. Why do you think humility is one of the marks of wisdom?
- Give an example of a time when your partner's apology was an encouragement to you.
- Talk about how the two of you deal with apologies. Do you have your own unique styles of saying "I'm sorry"?
- Sometimes a person will offer a premature apology—without true sorrow—just to put an end to discomfort. Have you ever been caught in this trap? How can you avoid it?
- How can the two of you more effectively pursue the habit of humility in your marriage? Be specific.

SOUL TO SOUL

To deepen your spiritual intimacy this next week, make note of:

- What you gained from this session together.
- A pressure point in your partner's upcoming week you will pray about.
- A concrete kindness you can offer your partner this week.

PRAYER

O God of grace, overcome the darkness of our indifference with your light. Swap our pride with your humility. Exchange our self-interest with a genuine empathy for each other, and a spirit that seeks to understand our partner's point of view. May the peace that accompanies this kind of humility fill our hearts all week long. Amen.

Real-Life Soul Mates

When we were married, I had dreams of having devotions with Karolyn every morning at breakfast. We would read the Bible and pray together and begin our day with God. Soon I discovered that Karolyn was not a morning person. Doing anything in the early morning was a chore for her. My response was to resent her and question her commitment to God. How foolish of me! I was trying to force her into my idea of spirituality.

So I meet and talk with God early each morning, and she checks in with God later in the morning. Then we check in with each other over lunch or via phone later in the day.

We share this to say that what works for one couple may not work for all couples.

One way we share our spiritual journey is to read to each other things we discover in the Scriptures or in the books we are reading. We also remind each other of people for whom we need to pray.

Karolyn will read of a need on Facebook and share it with me, or I will hear something at the office and share it with her. I serve on a church staff, so we attend lots of church dinners. For many years we have made it a practice to sit at different tables. Karolyn says jokingly, "We get more gossip when we do this." Actually, it gives us twice as much information to guide our prayers.

We also enjoy visiting our members who are no longer physically able to attend church. Touching those who sometimes are forgotten has been very rewarding to us.

In order to stay young, we try to hang out with young people as often as possible. Last night we drove an hour to visit with our high school students who are attending summer camp. We met with the counselors and also encouraged the cooks.

We are so grateful to be part of a local church family where so many good things are happening every week. We believe few things are more important than getting involved in a church where each of you can use your abilities and gifts to enhance the lives of others.

Gary and Karolyn Chapman

WHEN STRESS STRIKES YOUR MARRIAGE

It is 7:00 a.m., the start of another working day. Bleary-eyed from too little sleep, you drink a cup of coffee on your way out the door. Suddenly you remember that this evening it is your turn to host a couple's Bible study, so you frantically try to straighten up the house. You leave a few dishes in the sink and jump into your car to join the rest of the workforce in rush-hour traffic. Ten minutes into your commute, however, you realize that the report you worked on last night is still on your nightstand. You have no option but to drive back and retrieve it.

Late for work, you open your office door and find the boss pacing inside. Your report was due an hour ago, you are told; the client is furious. Your heart begins to race. Your palms begin to sweat. And you would like nothing more than to run away.

Instead, you swallow the primal urge and try to explain yourself. Your boss grabs the report from your outstretched hand. "This better not happen again," he warns. You slump into your chair and fumble through the bottom drawer of your desk for a bottle of aspirin. Your stomach is churning, your back muscles knotting, your blood pressure climbing.

This stress response is the same experience our ancestors had when suddenly faced with a saber-toothed tiger—a pounding heart, tense muscles, and a desperate urge to fight or flee. And while the ancient threat of a hungry tiger may be gone, the modern jungle is no less perilous.

And since fighting or fleeing is not really an option in the civilized world, our body's natural reaction to stress has no outlet. As a result we suffer from ulcers, high blood pressure, and other physical symptoms. But that's not all. We carry the stress of the workaday world into our marriage. The fight-or-flight response, if not properly managed, creates tension in our partnership. If we can't take out our anger on the boss, for example, we might take it out on our spouse.

So what do we do? Extinguish all stress? No. Too little stress can be just as damaging as too much. The ideal goal is balance. Somewhere between the fight-or-flight spasms of too much tension and the dullness of too little, the challenge for each person and each couple is to find the level of manageable stress that invigorates life instead of ravaging it. Physical activity and calming techniques help a lot. But the only sure way to prevent your stress from becoming debilitating is to respond to the call of Christ when he says, "Come to me . . . and I will give you rest" (Matt. 11:28). From the very beginning, rest has had a special significance for God: "Then God blessed the seventh day and made it holy, because on it he rested" (Gen. 2:3).

The most frequently overlooked dimension in stress management, even among Christians, is resting in God's presence. This is not always easy, mind you. Even the great leader Moses had difficulty with it. He experienced unrelieved stress trying to keep two million Israelites happy as they wandered in the wilderness.

In exasperation, Moses turned to God, pleading: "Why have you brought this trouble on your servant? . . . I cannot carry all these people by myself; the burden is too heavy for me." But God called Moses to rest in God's wisdom, and soon his burden and his stress became more manageable (see Num. 11:11–17). The same God who called Moses to rest calls you and your partner to relax with each other in his peace.

FROM GOD'S WORD

Do not be anxious about anything, but in every situation, by prayer and petition, with thanksgiving, present your requests to God. And the peace of God, which transcends all understanding, will guard your hearts and minds in Christ Jesus.

PHILIPPIANS 4:6–7

YOUR TURN

- What are you anxious about? Are you able to present it to God? If not, why not?
- Talk about how the two of you relax as individuals. What do each of you do to manage stress?
- Give an example of a recent stress outside your marriage that placed tension in your relationship. How does this happen, and what can you do to diminish it?
- Discuss the current pace of your lives. If you are like most people, you are often stressed out. What can you do this week to slow down?
- What is one thing you can each do for the other that will alleviate stress?

SOUL TO SOUL

To deepen your spiritual intimacy this next week, make note of:

- What you gained from this session together.
- A pressure point in your partner's upcoming week you will pray about.
- A concrete kindness you can offer your partner this week.

PRAYER

Lord God, you invited us to come to you to find rest. Help us together to still and quiet our souls in your presence. Grant us the wisdom to find a balanced lifestyle of challenge and rest that invigorates each of us without robbing us of joy. Amen.

Real-Life Soul Mates

When we were in our courtship phase, there were many things we discussed that were a bit foreign to each other. Things we did in each of our own individual lives that the other did not do in theirs. One of these was observing a day of rest.

Honoring the Sabbath was a commitment Fawn made to God long before we met. She didn't care so much if it happened Friday at sundown to Saturday at sundown, all day Saturday, or all day Sunday. The only thing she cared is at some point between the beginning of the week and the end, we paused for a day of rest. No work. No talk of work.

Although I didn't fully appreciate the importance of keeping the Sabbath, and had heard the argument on both sides as to whether it was still required as one of the original Ten Commandments or if it was no longer required after Christ came, what I knew is that Sabbath was important to her, so it became important to me.

At first, it was brutal. Incredibly tough to do. I was accustomed to working seven days a week and my colleagues, even though most are Jewish, didn't quite understand why I (a non-Jew) honored the Sabbath when most of them had long stopped even thinking about it. Then, over time, I realized that whether Sabbath was religiously required or not, it was absolutely brilliant for connecting with each other and connecting with God as one unit.

There are several benefits we experience as a result of honoring the Sabbath together each week:

Our available "balance" is increased. Like a bank account, if you are constantly withdrawing and giving to others, you will be left without anything to give. This day of rest gave us time to replenish our account so it was, once again, available for withdrawals without running the risk of overdrawing.

Our level of patience and tolerance increased. When we are rested and full of life, we respond to each other with a much greater level of grace.

Our energy is renewed. Every week, by the end of our Sabbath, all the energy and life the world has taken from us throughout the week is restored.

Our marriage is strengthened. Setting aside a day each week for "me" time, "us" time, and "anything that floats our boat" time allows us to stay connected.

We are happier. Happiness is a natural by-product of gratitude. When you slow your world down for an entire day to live intentionally, gratitude will find its way in and that complaining gremlin will find its way out.

Keith and Fawn Weaver

Session Twenty-Four

DESPERATELY SEEKING SCRIPTURE

We must have forty or fifty Bibles. They are of all sizes and colors—the King James, the New King James, the Good News, the New American Standard, the Amplified, the Living, the Message, the New International Version, the New Revised Standard Bible, and on and on. And then we have the workbook editions, the pocket editions, the illustrated editions, and the devotional editions. We are especially fond of the NIV Couples' Devotional Bible. Most of these, most of the time, however, sit on a shelf in our study at home.

But there are two Bibles—our personal Bibles—that are very different. Mine is a simple NIV with a brown leather cover that, because of wear, is no longer affixed to the spine (Les gave it to me on December 14, 1979—our first Christmas as a dating couple). His is a bigger, black leather Thompson Chain Reference NIV with thumb indentions for quick reference. Hardly a day goes by when these familiar books go unopened.

How about you? Do you make time to study God's Word? Have you discovered the beauty of Bible reading? One of the best descriptions of the Bible we have ever read came from old-time evangelist and professional baseball player Billy Sunday. In his book *The Man and His Message*, he talked about entering the "wonderful temple" of the Bible:

I entered at the portico of Genesis, walked down through the Old Testament art galleries, where pictures of Noah, Abraham, Moses, Joseph, Isaac, Jacob, and Daniel hung on the wall. I passed into the music room of Psalms, where the Spirit swept the key-board of nature until it seemed that every reed and pipe in God's great organ responded to the tuneful harp of David, the sweet singer of Israel. I entered the chamber of Ecclesiastes, where the voice of the preacher was heard; and into the conservatory of Sharon, where the Lily of the Valley's sweet-scented spices filled and perfumed my life. I entered the business office of Proverbs, and then into the observatory room of the Prophets, where I saw telescopes of various sizes, pointed to far-off events, but all concentrated upon the bright and morning star.

I entered the audience room of the King of Kings, and caught a vision of His glory from the standpoint of Matthew, Mark, Luke, and John, passed into the Acts of the Apostles, where the Holy Spirit was doing His work in the formation of the infant church. Then into the correspondence room, where sat Paul, Peter, James, and John, penning their epistles. I stepped into the throne room of Revelation, where towered the glittering peaks, and got a vision of the King sitting upon the throne in all His glory, and I cried:

"All hail the power of Jesus' name, Let angels prostrate fall
Bring forth the royal diadem,
And crown him Lord of all."

If you and your partner read the Bible individually, on your own throughout each week, your souls will be nourished and your marriage will be blessed (see Ps. 19:11; Matt. 7:24; Luke 11:28; John 5:24; 8:31; Rev. 1:3). For you will have the Word of God written on your hearts (see Deut. 6:6; Ps. 119:11).

FROM GOD'S WORD

Let the message of Christ dwell among you richly as you teach and admonish one another with all wisdom through psalms, hymns, and songs from the Spirit, singing to God with gratitude in your hearts.

Colossians 3:16

YOUR TURN

- Many people feel guilty for not spending more time reading the Bible. Do you ever struggle with consistent study of the Scripture?
- Does Bible study come more naturally to one of you than the other? This is not uncommon. What can you do to learn from each other?
- We all have our own devotional style. Describe to your partner how you go about your personal study time in the Word.
- Give an example of a time when Scripture encouraged or influenced you at a critical point in your life.
- How has your marriage been blessed and nourished by reading the Word of God?

SOUL TO SOUL

To deepen your spiritual intimacy this next week, make note of:

- What you gained from this session together.
- A pressure point in your partner's upcoming week you will pray about.
- A concrete kindness you can offer your partner this week.

PRAYER

Our Savior, you have given us your Word as our resource for life. Your Word revives our souls. It improves our wisdom, gives us joy, and fills our minds with greater light. May our marriage reap the great rewards promised for those who study and live by your Word. Thank you for the marvelous gift of Scripture. Amen.

Real-Life Soul Mates

Because Cathy and I were Christians when we married, we simply expected spiritual growth and spiritual intimacy to happen easily. How wrong we were! We tried the "roller coaster" devotional method for several years, and our daily devotions gradually shifted to a few times a month. Reading books together promised to change the situation, but we never made it through even one. We felt guilty that we weren't growing together. We were better at discipling teenagers in the youth group than we were at discipling each other.

Then we finally developed a spiritual tool that works for us. We call it "Jim and Cathy's weekly meeting." Although we pray with our children daily and with each other more than weekly, this weekly meeting has become the cornerstone for our spiritual intimacy as a couple. It's simple. We enjoy our devotional time for the week; we share our greatest joy, our greatest struggle, an affirmation, a wish or hope, and physical goals; we pray; and we discuss a book of the month. There are days when this takes us fifteen minutes, but we have also had marathon meetings for three hours.

Jim and Cathy Burns

Session Twenty-Five

HELP! WE NEED SOMEBODY!

Chances are that just this week you and your partner had a situation that required negotiation and compromise—a money matter came up, a conflict in household chores arose, or a discrepancy over discretionary time raised its head. And chances are that you quickly worked out a solution.

But truth be known, you and your spouse might encounter issues that aren't easily solved. Some stubborn problems come up time and again that you won't be able to work out on your own. And chances are, sooner or later, you'll need outside help to reach a resolution. So if that time arises, be ready. Make a commitment to each other now that you will seek the necessary help when you need it.

Oh, we know it never feels good to ask someone else for help. But seeking counsel is never a sign of weakness. Proverbs affirms this kind of help again and again: "Let the wise listen and add to their learning, and let the discerning get guidance" (1:5); "Plans fail for lack of counsel, but with many advisers they succeed" (15:22); "Instruct the wise and they will be wiser still; teach the righteous and they will add to their learning" (9:9).

125

Maybe you are thinking that you will never need a counselor because God can speak directly to you. That's true. But more often than not, God counsels us through the wisdom of other people, individuals who are wise, gifted, and trained to administer his healing.

How do you know when it is time to turn to a sensitive pastor or a professional counselor? Our friend Everett Worthington, in *Hope for Troubled Marriages*, lists several situations which indicate that a couple should consider seeing a counselor. Here are a few from his list: You are locked in a power struggle, someone is deeply depressed, alcohol or drug dependency has entered the marriage, sexual difficulties (impotence or premature ejaculation) have become a strain on the relationship, someone is suffering damage to their self-esteem, either of you is unable to forgive a past transgression, commitment to the marriage is wearing thin, your marital tensions are snowballing quickly. These are just a few of the indicators Everett notes. The bottom line is that if you think you need marriage counseling, you probably do.

What should you look for in a good counselor? If the counselor is not your pastor, we suggest that you explore his or her beliefs and values (are they in sync with yours?). You will also want to know about the counselor's training and education. But one of the most important things to do in finding a competent counselor is to get a good referral. Ask around. Word of mouth is often the best way to find someone who will really help.

Chances are that you are doing a pretty good job of solving your problems yourselves. But if the time comes when you need something more, remember that while Christ is the ultimate Counselor (see Isa. 9:6), the servants of Christ that work in counseling offices and pastor's studies are often a conduit for administering his help. So "listen to advice and accept discipline, and at the end you will be counted among the wise" (Prov. 19:20).

FROM GOD'S WORD

But the Advocate, the Holy Spirit, whom the Father will send in my
name, will teach you all things and will remind you of everything
I have said to you.

JOHN 14:26

YOUR TURN

- Why is seeking guidance so crucial to acquiring the
  wisdom that leads to a fulfilled life?
- Give an example of a time when advice, insight, or
  counsel from a trusted source facilitated growth in you or
  your marriage relationship.
- Identify an experienced, healthy couple you might invite to
  mentor you as a couple. What do you think about this idea?
- Take an inventory of your relationship. Are there any
  red flags that might alert you to the need for marriage
  counseling? How can you be sure you are being honest
  about your real needs?
- What can you do in a concrete way to ensure that you will
  seek help if and when it is necessary for your marriage?

SOUL TO SOUL

To deepen your spiritual intimacy this next week, make note of:

- What you gained from this session together.
- A pressure point in your partner's upcoming week you
  will pray about.
- A concrete kindness you can offer your partner this week.

PRAYER

Our Father, we recognize our need for help. Give us teachable spirits and keep us sensitive to the counsel of your Holy Spirit. And save us from the fear of seeking special help from qualified people when we need it. Thank you for your great love. Amen.

Real-Life Soul Mates

We've only been married five years, so it's hard to imagine having a lot of wisdom to share. But certain building blocks have given us a solid foundation in these early years.

The first is a shared purpose in ministry. We first met at the University of Tennessee, where we served as leaders in a ministry called Young Life. The mission of Young Life revolves around sharing the heart of Jesus with high school students, so we were spending our free time helping teens in the Knoxville area. That passion has carried over into our marriage and has unified us in these early years.

Next, we've made it a priority to involve older couples in our lives. Sometimes these relationships are called "mentorships," but they go so much deeper for us. We have been blessed to also call them "friendships." We've really learned the importance of staying accountable to each other and having older, wiser couples speak into our lives at every level.

We also haven't been afraid to seek counseling. About three years into our marriage, we were hung up on a couple of issues. We really needed a third party to help us work through our differences, and we came out of that experience refined and unified.

Counseling often comes with a stigma, but I'm so glad we didn't let that hold us back. Marriage is hard work and creates some difficult situations. Having someone walk with us and ask us the hard questions honestly changed the course of our lives.

Finally, we've made serving one another a priority. Over the past two years, we've discovered that serving each other eliminates so many small, picky things that can whittle away at a marriage.

We just had our first child, Amelia. God has used her as another catalyst in our family's spiritual journey. Since her birth, we've been praying that she'll find God early in life and follow him with all her heart. This new life God has entrusted to us also gives us an even deeper appreciation for how God loves each of us.

We believe the first few years set the tone in a marriage. If you can work through the hard things and set up healthy habits, you can foster a deeper love for each other. And it's easier to establish positive habits in the first three years of marriage than to try to repair the damage after thirty years.

We know we have so much more to learn, but we're thankful for the foundation God has provided so far.

Winston and Rachel Cruze

Session Twenty-Six

FIGHTING THE GOOD FIGHT

Conflict is a natural component of every marriage. No matter how deeply a man and woman love each other, they will encounter conflict. Thirty-seven percent of newlyweds admit to being more critical of their mates after marriage. And 30 percent report an increase in arguments after the honeymoon.

Whether you argue does not determine the health of your marriage. Far more important than how often you argue is *how* you argue. Dr. John Gottman of the University of Washington has been studying marriages for more than twenty years, and he has identified the signs in conflict that almost always spell disaster. He calls them "The Four Horsemen of the Apocalypse." And when they gallop into your relationship, danger is imminent. In a continuum from least to most dangerous, the four horsemen are: criticism, contempt, defensiveness, and stonewalling.

Do these characteristics describe your quarrels? Be on the lookout. Criticism, of course, often comes into play in marital spats, but when it leads to contempt—when sarcasm and name-calling enter the picture—you are on a slippery slope. At the risk of oversimplifying Gottman's findings, you might think of a destructive argument as one that resorts to belittling and degrading. When this happens, partners begin to focus on every past sin and failure of their spouse and aggressively whittle away at each other's dignity. This kind of arguing drives a wedge between couples. The next time they argue, the wedge will be driven farther and the division in their relationship made wider. After enough shouting matches, the pattern becomes ingrained and is likely to be settled ultimately in a divorce court.

To avoid the deadly trap of contempt, focus on the issue at hand—not your partner's character. If the problem is in-laws, for example, or how money is spent, or the use of personal time, argue about that, and stay away from personality assassination. You may disagree vehemently, but don't shut your partner out; don't roll your eyes in disgust. Stay on the issue and God will grant you patience and encouragement in a spirit of unity (see Rom. 15:5).

We'll say it again: Conflict is a natural part of building intimacy. So don't avoid differences. Don't bury your conflicts. Go ahead, fight. But keep your conflict restricted to the issues that really matter.

You've probably seen the "grant me the wisdom to accept the things I cannot change" prayer on plaques and posters. It may be trivialized by overfamiliarity, but it's true: One of the major tasks of marriage is learning what can and should be changed (habits of nagging, for example) and what should be over-looked (the fact that your in-laws are coming for Christmas). So remember this saying from Proverbs: "The words of the reckless pierce like swords, but the tongue of the wise brings healing" (12:18).

FROM GOD'S WORD

You have heard that it was said to the people long ago, "You shall not murder, and anyone who murders will be subject to judgment." But I tell you that anyone who is angry with a brother or sister will be subject to judgment. Again, anyone who says to his brother or sister, "Raca," [an Aramaic term of contempt] is answerable to the court. And anyone who says, "You fool!" will be in danger of the fire of hell. Therefore, if you are offering your gift at the altar and there remember that your brother or sister has something against you, leave your gift there in front of the altar. First go and be reconciled to them; then come and offer your gift.

MATTHEW 5:21–24

YOUR TURN

- Discuss the meaning of Christ's warning about the destructiveness of contempt in relationships. Why would he mention this?
- Give an example of a time when a disagreement strengthened your marriage—a time you were strengthened because of your honest admission of conflict.
- What have been your models for learning how to resolve conflicts? How did your parents fight?
- When it comes to difficult issues, what are the roles each of you tend to take? How can you learn from the strengths of the other?
- How can the two of you prepare in advance to make your next conflict a "good fight"? Talk about this in specific terms.

SOUL TO SOUL

To deepen your spiritual intimacy this next week, make note of:

- What you gained from this session together.
- A pressure point in your partner's upcoming week you will pray about.
- A concrete kindness you can offer your partner this week.

PRAYER

Teach us, O Lord, to disagree without a critical or contemptuous spirit. Lift us above the fear of conflict and allow our differences to strengthen one another as iron sharpens iron. Help us never to lose sight of our partner's true significance even in the shadow of disagreement. Bind us together through Jesus Christ our Lord. Amen.

Real-Life Soul Mates

Early in our marriage, Gail and I attended a church led by a dynamic, thirty-something pastor. He was an extraordinary communicator and a wise and empathetic counselor. As a result, the church grew rapidly.

But as we got better acquainted with him and his wife, we started noticing a disturbing trend in the way they related to one another. They would often make disparaging remarks about the other in public.

At first it seemed cute. Their comments seemed playful and humorous. Everyone laughed. But over time, they became more and more pointed, thinly masking their frustration with one another.

We ultimately left that church. But several years later we learned they suffered an ugly divorce, with both admitting to multiple affairs. They lost their family, and, of course, their ministry. To this day, it grieves me to think about it.

Conversely, I noticed that my mentor, Sam Moore, always spoke highly of his wife. He would often say, "I hate to leave her in the morning, and I can't wait to see her in the evening." They have been married now for nearly sixty years. Last time Gail and I were with them, they were holding hands, obviously still in love.

In reflecting on these two experiences, I am convinced that praising your spouse in public is one of the most important investments you can make—and believe it or not, we've found that it helps us cultivate spiritual intimacy in our marriage.

Here's what we've learned about affirmation and how it joins our spirits:

You get more of what you affirm. Have you ever noticed that when someone praises you, you want to repeat the behavior that caused it?

Affirmation shifts your attitude toward each other. Words are powerful tools. They can create, or they can destroy. If you start speaking well of your spouse, you start believing what you say.

Affirmation helps strengthen your spouse's best qualities. Encouragement is also a powerful force for good.

Affirmation wards off the temptation of adultery. When others see you are happily married, they are less likely to proposition you. It's like a hedge that protects your marriage from would-be predators.

Affirming your spouse is an investment that pays big dividends. And it's sure to help you join your spirits together.

Michael and Gail Hyatt

Session Twenty-Seven

A KISS
ON THE LIPS

Rebecca and Steve, very much in love, had been married only a few weeks when she cooked eggplant lasagna. She asked Steve if he liked it. Steve knew Rebecca had worked hard to make it and was afraid that he would offend her if he was honest. "Oh yes," he told Rebecca, "it's great!" But he hated it. Believing that Steve really liked it, Rebecca began cooking the dish quite regularly. Since she had difficulty breaking down the recipe, there was always a great quantity of leftovers, so the lasagna appeared many times during the week. Finally Steve could bear it no longer and, in a moment of anger, he confessed that he hated her cooking, that it gagged him, and that he never wanted to see eggplant lasagna on his table again! Rebecca was shocked and hurt. He had *lied* to her. In tears she said, "I'll never believe you again!"

The tragedy of most seemingly insignificant experiences of deception is that they grow, and ultimately cast a shadow of distrust over a relationship. That's why Solomon wrote, "An honest answer is like a kiss on the lips" (Prov. 24:26).

Soul mates must have integrity. Without it, Scripture says, we will be despised and destroyed (see Ps. 5:6; 63:11; 101:7; Prov. 11:3; 12:8; 19:1; Rev. 21:8). Integrity means telling the truth, keeping our promises, doing what we said we would do, choosing to be accountable, and taking as our motto *semper fidelis*—the promise to be *always faithful*.

"If I *always* tell the truth," you may be saying, "won't I hurt my partner's feelings?" No. Truth is "brutal" only when it is a partial truth or when it is meant to cause pain. If, for example, Leslie asks me if I like the banana bread she made, I could say, "Yuck! I can't stand it." But would that be the truth? Only part of it. It would be more completely honest to say, "Not really, I've never liked banana bread—but it doesn't make a bit of difference to me, this meal is still good." When Paul wrote to the church he began in Thessalonica (Acts 17:1–9), he said, "For the appeal we make does not spring from error or impure motives, nor are we trying to trick you. On the contrary, we speak as those approved by God to be entrusted with the gospel. We are not trying to please people but God, who tests our hearts" (1 Thess. 2:3–4). That is the key to "speaking the truth in love" (Eph. 4:15)—not to trick or manipulate, but to love our spouse and to please God.

Honesty, as a popular song says, is such a lonely word. At times it does seem that everyone is so untrue. And it's been that way for a long time. Consider these verses: "Everyone is a liar" (Ps. 116:11); "Friend deceives friend, and no one speaks the truth" (Jer. 9:5). The book of Proverbs asks, "Many claim to have unfailing love, but a faithful person who can find?" (20:6). The gift of integrity is so rare. But doesn't your marriage deserve it?

So kiss your spouse on the lips with honesty. He or she will say with the psalmist, "The law from your mouth is more precious to me than thousands of pieces of silver and gold" (119:72).

FROM GOD'S WORD

Therefore, since through God's mercy we have this ministry, we do not lose heart. Rather, we have renounced secret and shameful ways; we do not use deception, nor do we distort the word of God. On the contrary, by setting forth the truth plainly we commend ourselves to everyone's conscience in the sight of God.

2 CORINTHIANS 4:1–2

YOUR TURN

- In your opinion, why is truth so fundamental to love? Can you have love without truth?
- How have you struggled with being truthful (a desire to protect, a propensity to exaggerate, a tendency to control or to avoid a conflict, etc.)?
- Give an example of a time when you benefited from an honest, if painful, answer from someone. How did it help you?
- What experiences have you shared that have strengthened and developed the trust between you?
- How can you work together more effectively to "speak the truth in love"?

SOUL TO SOUL

To deepen your spiritual intimacy this next week, make note of:

- What you gained from this session together.
- A pressure point in your partner's upcoming week you will pray about.
- A concrete kindness you can offer your partner this week.

PRAYER

Gracious God, help us to give ourselves to the task of developing personal integrity—especially in all our ordinary conversations this week. Teach us how to be honest without hurting anyone. Release us from the compulsion to trick, manipulate, or protect our spouse from the truth. Amen.

Real-Life Soul Mates

Our relationship books unexpectedly became worldwide bestsellers when our kids were toddlers, and our pattern of how we did spiritual life together as a couple changed dramatically. We suddenly went from having a busy-but-normal schedule that included regular time to pray together, to an unpredictable and chaotic schedule with lots of travel. Our idealistic notion of a predictable pattern of marital spiritual activity went out the window—and it might be one of the best things that could have happened for our spiritual life as a couple and a family.

You see, we never did those idealistic, just-the-two-of-us spiritual activities as regularly as we wanted *anyway*. We were always very purposeful about personal prayer and Bible study, attending church, and hosting a married couples' small group in our home, so we had good teaching, worship, and fellowship with others. All that was crucial for our growth as a couple. But although we also wanted regular marital devotions, it often got pushed aside for one thing or another.

Suddenly, with the advent of our unpredictable schedule, we realized: since we can't *schedule* prayer time, we have to *grab* prayer time. We began looking at prayer in a new way. When there was a need, we stopped and prayed right then. No putting it on the list to pray about it that night—because we might not *have* a joint prayer time that night.

We also began looking at devotions and discussion in a new way. Instead of creating a set time and piece of content to work through together, we began to share more about what God might be saying to us through our personal Bible reading, the pastoral podcast Jeff was listening to, or something Shaunti's friend told her in Bible study as part of our regular conversations with each other—and later, with the kids.

Our kids have rarely seen us do a marital devotion together, but every day they hear us talk about what God might want us to learn from this dicey situation at school or from that Bible verse that perplexes us. Every day they see us stop and pray right when there is a need. And every night, we tuck each of them in and pray more officially for what is on their hearts.

These moments are snatched . . . but our prayer is that God will use these purposeful moments to draw *all* of us closer to him—even in the midst of the beautiful chaos of life.

Jeff and Shaunti Feldhahn

HOW IRON SHARPENS IRON

When researchers asked husbands and wives, "What is it you've gotten out of marriage?" couples often said something like, "My partner has shown me parts of my personality I didn't know were there." In other words, marriage heightened my self-awareness and has helped me to grow.

Personal growth is one of the fringe benefits of a good marriage. Having a spouse, in a sense, is like having an intimate mirror that reflects who you really are and, as a result, provides more opportunities for personal change. That's why research shows that married people are healthier on nearly every spectrum than the rest of the population. That is also why Scripture says, "He [or she] who finds a wife [or husband] finds what is good and receives favor from the LORD" (Prov. 18:22).

Marriage comes with a built-in reality check. We ask questions of our partner such as, "Do you think I came across too flippant when John asked me about my job?" Or, "Do you think I don't smile very much?" And sometimes our partner says things such as, "Honey, you do tend to jump to conclusions at times." Or "Do you realize how much you worry about that?" Questions and comments like these emerge naturally in a healthy marriage, and they become the stimulus for personal change.

Everyone needs to grow. No one has become all he or she can be. Even the apostle Paul said, "Not that I have already obtained all this, or have already arrived at my goal, but I press on to take hold of that for which Christ Jesus took hold of me" (Phil. 3:12).

Of course, change isn't easy. Take the configuration of the letters on a computer keyboard as an illustration. Back in the 1870s, a manufacturer of typewriters received complaints about the typewriter keys sticking together if the user went too fast. Engineers for the company decided that the best way to keep the keys from jamming was to slow the operator down. So they developed a more inefficient keyboard with letters like O and I (two of the most frequently used letters in the alphabet) positioned for the relatively weaker ring and little fingers. Depressing these keys simply took more time. The problem was solved, no more jammed keys. Since the time of that solution, however, typing technology and word processing have advanced significantly. Today's electric typewriters and word processors can go much faster than any human can type. The problem is that we don't want to change the keyboard—even though it would help us type faster.

Change is hard. But don't allow that to stand in the way of pinpointing something you need to change about yourself. Ask for feedback from your spouse and, with his or her help, devise a personal plan for improvement. You and your partner can help each other become self-aware and your marriage will be the better for it. "As iron sharpens iron," Proverbs says, "so one person sharpens another" (27:17).

FROM GOD'S WORD

And he said: "Truly I tell you, unless you change and become like little children, you will never enter the kingdom of heaven. Therefore, whoever takes the lowly position of this child is the greatest in the kingdom of heaven."

MATTHEW 18:3–4

YOUR TURN

- How do you incorporate the process of personal change into your spiritual pilgrimage? How does God speak to you about things you need to change?
- Has being married increased your level of self-awareness? If so, in what ways?
- Share with your partner the desires you have for personal improvement.
- Give an example of a time when your partner's feedback helped produce a positive change in you.
- What can you do to more effectively promote growth in one another? In other words, how can you "sharpen" each other?

SOUL TO SOUL

To deepen your spiritual intimacy this next week, make note of:

- What you gained from this session together.
- A pressure point in your partner's upcoming week you will pray about.
- A concrete kindness you can offer your partner this week.

PRAYER

Our Father in heaven, grant unto us the courage, grace, and strength to look into the mirror of our partner's eyes and listen attentively to his or her speech, so we may clearly understand the ways we may improve our side of the relationship. Complete your work in us so that we reflect your image. Amen.

Real-Life Soul Mates

There is something powerful and poignant about couples sitting together, sharing their hearts with one another, and talking and listening to the Lord as husband and wife. Life's challenges are more easily seen in a healthy perspective when couples sit in his presence.

Taking time to read the Bible and pray together is a commitment Jean and I made early on in our marriage. In one sense, it was the easiest and most refreshing part of our day. It was a chance to unwind from our responsibilities and to reconnect with one another and with the Lord.

But years into our relationship there came a moment when we realized we weren't spending that time together very often, and we had to ask ourselves why. We found that we had entered a season of life where our focus had shifted away from each other and toward our boys' needs and their spiritual development.

Most Christian parents can relate. Our days are full getting the kids back and forth to school, athletic practice, and doctor and dentist appointments. Then there's the homework, bath times, and, of course, the full-time jobs we work every day. It's difficult to keep all of those plates spinning.

In our case, once we had read to our boys, prayed with them, and talked with them about their day, Jean and I would fall into bed exhausted. Reading and praying with each other felt like just one more thing to do.

But we knew our spiritual health as a couple didn't only benefit our marriage; it was crucial to the well-being of our family. We recognized that our boys will thrive, not because we're directing all of our energy toward them, but first and foremost because Jean and I have built a strong, healthy marriage.

So we have recommitted to praying together after the kids have gone to bed for the evening. It hasn't been easy, and we aren't able to do it every night. But we have made it a priority to be consistent.

And you know what? It's been a wonderful experience that has paid big dividends in our household. Not only have Jean and I been drawn closer together as a couple, but it's also bonded us even more firmly to our boys.

Jim and Jean Daly

Session Twenty-Nine

THE IMPORTANCE OF SAYING "I LOVE YOU"

Emily sat in our office weeping. She came for counseling on her own, without telling her husband. "I am so hungry for affection," she confided in us. "We have been married for twenty-five years, and I know he is capable of tenderness. He shows it to the dog. But . . ." Emily's voice broke down and her tears began to flow. She reached for a tissue and quietly said, " . . . I'd just like to hear him say, 'I love you.'"

Three simple words. So critical to marriage. We take these tender words for granted sometimes, but we have never known anyone who got tired of hearing "I love you" . . . before leaving the house in the morning . . . after a quick message on the answering machine . . . while working in the garden . . . before dozing off in bed. These little words are like nutrients to a marriage. Without a consistent dose of verbal expression, without saying and hearing those words, the soul of a marriage withers.

Think about it. We have over six hundred thousand words in the English language and more synonyms per word than are found in any other language. However, we have only one word with which to express all the various shadings of love. Deficient as English is in this respect, we long to hear the familiar words, "I love you."

Again and again, your spouse needs to hear the words. And, by the way, it is just as important for you to say them. At the university where we work there is a sophisticated voice mail system on our phones. One of the features is called "future delivery." It enables a person to record a message to someone and then specify the time and date they want the message delivered. One day I (Les) got the idea of sending Leslie several "I love you" messages on her phone. *Why not do a bunch of them now while I'm thinking about it*, I thought to myself. As a Type-A, I was excited to be so loving and check it off my to-do list at the same time. So I recorded my tender messages one after the next and then sent them "future delivery" on different days throughout the coming month. Leslie, not knowing what I had done, believed she was receiving spontaneous, loving messages from her husband every few days. And all I had to do was sit back and let my voice mail do my romancing. Funny thing, however. While Leslie, none the wiser, loved my messages, I began to feel phony. Saying "I love you," for me, was starting to fall into the same category as paying the bills. Well, needless to say, I haven't put my love on "future delivery" since. My sneaky scheme, however, taught me something important—I need to say "I love you" as much as Leslie needs to hear it.

The poet W. H. Auden remarked, "We must love one another or die!" He is surely right. A marriage cannot survive without verbal expressions of love. So pray that the Lord will "make your love increase and overflow for each other" (1 Thess. 3:12).

FROM GOD'S WORD

Love is patient, love is kind. It does not envy, it does not boast, it is not proud. It does not dishonor others, it is not self-seeking, it is not easily angered, it keeps no record of wrongs. Love does not delight in evil but rejoices with the truth. It always protects, always trusts, always hopes, always perseveres. Love never fails.

1 Corinthians 13:4–8

YOUR TURN

- How do you make your love "overflow" for each other? Does your faith influence your expressions of love?
- How was love expressed in your family while growing up? How often were the words *I love you* used?
- Is it more difficult for one or both of you to express loving words routinely? Why or why not?
- Tell about a recent incident when you were especially appreciative of your partner saying "I love you."
- What can you and your partner do to cultivate a free exchange of loving messages in your relationship?

SOUL TO SOUL

To deepen your spiritual intimacy this next week, make note of:

- What you gained from this session together.
- A pressure point in your partner's upcoming week you will pray about.
- A concrete kindness you can offer your partner this week.

PRAYER

O God, our Father, teach us to open the doors to tenderness by freely saying to each other, "I love you." Open our mouths, unstop our ears, and illumine our eyes to the many ways we can be healing reminders of your love to one another. May loving words fill our home and empower our marriage. Amen.

Real-Life Soul Mates

Like many second marriages, ours came from pain. I had recently lost my wife of forty-two years in a hard-fought, six-year battle with cancer. Rosemary's husband had left her and her four children approximately two decades earlier.

I had not "dated" or "courted" in the formal sense, for decades. And we did not know each other during our previous marriages. We were—to put it bluntly—strangers. The decisions we made *before* and *as* we met laid the foundation for future enjoyed intimacy. Allow me to explain.

Rosemary selected the place of our first meeting—a thoughtfully chosen gazebo. In so doing, she was saying, "This is important."

As a man in my sixties, I was going on—now this was a bit scary—a "first date." A group of women—including my daughters, my mother, and my sister—helped to prepare me for the date. Yes, they even insisted on manicures and pedicures!

And as I flew to her city to meet her, I rented a brand new white Mercedes for the occasion. The selection of the make of the car was not to impress her. It was to say, "I want you to be honored." And the reason for choosing a white one? So that she could say that "he came riding in on a white horse!" You might be chuckling, but I was serious. We both wanted to convey to each other, "You are special."

I was instructed by my enthusiastic "Courtship Team" to buy a special cologne. I did. I was told to buy a new tie. I did. For one reason: to say "you are valued!"

Since our first date would be followed by Rosemary being gone to Israel (as I write this she is planning her fifty-fourth trip to Israel) and Turkey for six weeks, imagine my shock when—as we said goodbye—she said, "Can I take the tie and the cologne with me—to remember you and our first date?" My male response was twofold: (1) Why would anybody want my tie and cologne? But (2) I'm sure glad she asked for it.

You get the picture. The relationship began with "how can I show her how treasured and valued she is?" And she treated me the same way. That "holding in high esteem" formed the foundation of what would be a second marriage for both of us. And it has continued.

I still say multiple times a day, "Since we arrived here (assuming we are going somewhere), have I told you that I love you?" Or if we are leaving on a plane, "Since the plane took off, have I told you that I love you?" Or if we are arriving home, "Since we arrived home, have I told you that I love you?" This honoring treatment of a spouse prepares the way for intimacy.

Jim and Rosemary Garlow

IN SICKNESS
AND IN HEALTH

Leslie had the flu a week ago. I can't stand it when she's sick. I feel so helpless, like I can't do a thing in the world to make her feel any better. I run to the store and pick up a bottle of 7-Up and some soda crackers. This last time I bought a couple of different kinds of flu medicine. "That's so sweet," she said to me as she sat up on the couch wrapped in a blanket.

Okay, I thought to myself, *it will be another day or so and she'll be up and at 'em.* But she wasn't. For the rest of the week she stayed in bed, sipping 7-Up from a straw and complaining that the house was too cold, then too hot, then too cold. *What am I supposed to do now?* I wondered. I called our doctor. He said the flu was going around and all Leslie needed was bed rest. Ugh! I wanted to do something so I wouldn't feel so helpless. I guess that's why I enjoy stories of couples whose love has survived a time of serious illness. And I'm a sucker for any movie about tragic love.

But there is one real-life love story that invades my mind whenever Leslie gets sick. It puts my feelings of helplessness into perspective. In *Saving Your Marriage Before It Starts,* we told the story of Robertson McQuilkin and his wife Muriel, and it deserves repeating. The love he demonstrated for her when she was diagnosed with Alzheimer's disease is nothing less than extraordinary. Robertson was a college president who still had eight years to go before retirement. Muriel, once the host of a successful radio program, was experiencing tragic memory failure. She could not speak in sentences, only words, and often words that made little sense. But she could say one sentence, and she said it often: "I love you." While Robertson's friends urged him to arrange for the institutionalization of Muriel, he would not stand for it. "How could anyone love her the way I do?" asked Robertson.

Have you thought much about the part of your wedding vow that says, "To love and to honor in sickness and in health"? Robertson McQuilkin has. But not only has he thought about it, he's lived it. Believing that being faithful to Muriel "in sickness and in health" was a matter of integrity, Robertson McQuilkin resigned his presidency, and for the thirteen years of her decline he cared for his wife full-time.

Robertson understood the words of Christ when he said, "I needed clothes and you clothed me, I was sick and you looked after me" (Matt. 25:36). How about you? The next time your partner is ill, remember that it is an opportunity to put hands and feet to your marriage vows—in sickness and in health.

FROM GOD'S WORD

Jesus went through Galilee, teaching in their synagogues, proclaiming the good news of the kingdom, and healing every disease and sickness among the people.

MATTHEW 4:23

YOUR TURN

- Why do you think Christ ministered to the sick and the needy?
- What does "in sickness and in health" mean to you? How do you and will you live out this part of your marriage vow?
- Describe to your partner how you like to be treated when you are ill (doted on, left alone, etc.).
- How do you feel when your spouse is sick? Talk about the role of helping the sick partner. What is the toughest part?
- Give an example of a time when you were ill and the care of a parent or loved one was especially meaningful.

SOUL TO SOUL

To deepen your spiritual intimacy this next week, make note of:

- What you gained from this session together.
- A pressure point in your partner's upcoming week you will pray about.
- A concrete kindness you can offer your partner this week.

PRAYER

Gracious God, it is during the times when we are the most needy that you embrace us. When we are sick or hurting, may we turn to you, the Great Physician, for healing. Give us a gentle love and unfailing courage to be there for each other when we are suffering in body or spirit. Amen.

Real-Life Soul Mates

Ken opened the front door so I could wheel out to the van. It was the freshest of mornings. *O God*, I breathed, *if only I could feel as fresh.*

After four and a half decades of quadriplegia, I'm tired. My bones are weary and thin from battling everything from pressure sores to stage III cancer. My question these days is never "Why, God?" It's most often "How?" How do I keep on going? How can I be kind and civil when pain wracks me? How can I find the strength to face this day?

My husband, Ken, always seems to have the answer. "Why aren't you out by the van?" he asked when he came from the kitchen. Staring at the splendorous morning, I answered him with a sigh.

"Wait here," he said. "I know *exactly* what you need." He returned with a yellow post-it note on which he had scrawled the letter *C.* I gave him an odd look. "It stands for courage," he said, "the courage of Christ. I can see it in your eyes, Joni, and you can *do* this. I *know* you can!" With that, he pressed the post-it on my shirt. And grace flooded my heart with those few words of encouragement.

After thirty-three years of marriage, Ken has learned how to be strong when I am weak. And I have learned how to be strong when *he* is weak. Because of my quadriplegia, we both recognize that weakness is ingrained deeply into our marriage—it means we *must* think the best of each other, view the devil and not my disability as the enemy, and lean *very* hard on Jesus.

Proverbs 18:21 sums it up: "The tongue has the power of life and death." Ken said only a few words, and probably without giving them much thought. But those words were brimming with power and life. His was a pronouncement of the good he saw in me . . . or at least the good he *wanted* to see. And God made good on my husband's declaration.

It's a hard world. Even the best of marriages feel the weight of weariness. Little wonder husbands and wives are to "encourage one another daily" (Heb. 3:13). Whether you say it in an email, over the phone, or in person, your words to your spouse have the capacity to change their countenance and their character. Because even weakness in marriage has its strengths!

Ken and Joni Eareckson Tada

THE POWER OF LOVE IN ACTION

We have some friends who have been married more than thirty years. In their mid-fifties now, they seem to enjoy all the blessings possible for a healthy married couple—a beautiful home, good friends, bright children, and fulfilling careers. But their marriage hasn't been a walk on easy street. Their second child, a boy, was just four years old when he wandered into a neighbor's yard and drowned in their swimming pool.

The mother found her son facedown in the water and worked frantically to revive him, as did the emergency crew, but his life was lost. Faced with this tragedy and the unbearable grief that followed, this couple could have given up. After all, it is not uncommon for a marriage to dissolve in the face of overwhelming suffering. Strangely, sorrowful partners sometimes retreat to separate and bitter corners of misery. And because misery doesn't always love company, their circumstances tear them apart instead of bringing them together. But not this couple; they chose to call upon the power of love to help them weather their tragedy as partners.

Are you and your partner cultivating the power of love? We hope you will never be forced to test its strength, and we pray you will always rest in the courage that comes from a healthy Christian marriage. "Who shall separate us from the love of Christ? Shall trouble or hardship or persecution or famine or nakedness or danger or sword? . . . No, in all these things we are more than conquerors through him who loved us" (Rom. 8:35, 37).

In his book *Power through Constructive Thinking*, Emmet Fox wrote these words about the power of love:

> There is no difficulty that enough love will not conquer; no disease that enough love will not heal; no door that enough love will not open; no gulf that enough love will not bridge; no wall that enough love will not throw down; no sin that enough love will not redeem.
>
> It makes no difference how deeply seated may be the trouble, how hopeless the outlook, how muddled the tangle, how great the mistake, a sufficient realization of love will dissolve it all. If only you could love enough you would be the happiest and most powerful being in the world.

What a marvelous resource partners can be to one another. For as we cultivate love we strengthen our ability to cope with all that life might bring. And in the process we are reminded that "in all things God works for the good of those who love him" (Rom. 8:28).

FROM GOD'S WORD

I pray that out of his glorious riches he may strengthen you with power through his Spirit in your inner being, so that Christ may dwell in your hearts through faith. And I pray that you, being rooted and established in love, may have power, together with all the Lord's holy people, to grasp how wide and long and high and deep is the love of Christ.

EPHESIANS 3:16–18

YOUR TURN

- How do you experience the love of Christ in your life? When have you felt most loved by God?
- Give a personal example of a time when an unexpected or painful blow was mitigated by love in your life.
- Since misery doesn't always love company, what can you do now to ensure that when misery strikes your lives you will not be pulled apart?
- What can you do as a couple to cultivate a reliance on the power of God's love in times of difficulty?
- Do you agree with Emmet Fox that no matter how deep the trouble, a sufficient realization of love will dissolve it? Why or why not?

SOUL TO SOUL

To deepen your spiritual intimacy this next week, make note of:

- What you gained from this session together.
- A pressure point in your partner's upcoming week you will pray about.
- A concrete kindness you can offer your partner this week.

PRAYER

Dear God, sometimes the storms of life threaten to overcome our human capacity to love. Help us to drive our roots down deep, to be so established in your love that we might know its height and depth which surpasses understanding and be filled to overflowing with a measure of that love within our marriage—especially in the face of unexpected loss, bitter disappointments, and unsolvable situations. Amen.

Real-Life Soul Mates

My wife and I have come to see life more and more as a war. Ultimately, our battle is with the forces of evil, but on a daily level war involves a struggle with time, money, priorities, health, and unplanned crisis. If we are to fight as allies, then we must grow in greater intimacy. To this growth we devote our time before dinner. This time is sacred and rarely crowded out by other activities. It is our R and R to return to fighting well.

This has required repeated instructions to our children not to interrupt us. It requires us to let the phone ring, to let guests wait for their hosts to return, and to offend countless others who see that as a selfish venture. In fact, it is a refueling time that allows us to engage with our world with a dearer loyalty to one another, a deepened passion for what is good, and a sense of rest that can come from no other place.

The time is seldom less than a half hour and occasionally may stretch for an hour. We usually begin by catching up on the events of the day. Soon, the events become the springboard for conversation about what was provoked in us that caused distress or delight. Often my wife will have read or thought about things that she recorded in her journal, and she will read to me. Other times I will want her to listen to something I have written. We find it crucial to read out loud together: it not only crystallizes our vague struggles, but it also records our progress together through life.

Our time is unstructured, but it is not uncommon for us to move from events to feelings, from a struggle to joy, or from reading to prayer. In conclusion and consummation we call on God to deepen our heart for him. We return to our family and world refreshed in our sense of being intimate allies.

Dan and Rebecca Allender

AVOIDING THE BLAME GAME

Have you noticed lately that everyone seems to be a victim? The media has. The *New Yorker* magazine, for example, featured a cover story with the title, "The New Culture of Victimization," and the headline of the inside story was "Don't Blame Me!" On the cover of a *Time* magazine these words appeared: "Cry Babies and Eternal Victims!" *Esquire* followed with an article titled "A Confederacy of Complainers." It seems people these days don't want to be held accountable.

Take, for example, the FBI agent who embezzled two thousand dollars from the government and lost it in an afternoon of gambling in Atlantic City. He was fired, as he should have been, but he won a reinstatement to his post when the court ruled that he had a gambling handicap and was thus protected under federal law.

Or consider the man who applied for a job as a park attendant in Dane County, Wisconsin. A background check revealed that he had been convicted more than thirty times for flashing and indecent exposure. But when the park service turned him down, he sued them. He had never flashed in a park, only in libraries and laundromats, and thus employment officials determined that he should be hired because he had been a victim of job discrimination.

We will leave it to the social commentators to explain just how our new culture of victimization will affect society, but we know exactly how it can affect a marriage. Once a husband or wife becomes wrapped up in the blame game (blaming parents, genes, a boss, or a spouse, for example), a vicious cycle of shirked responsibility permeates the relationship. Soon each partner is looking for ways to avoid responsibility and shift the blame. Of course, this is nothing new. Ever since Adam blamed Eve, and Eve blamed the serpent, we have learned the trick of finding excuses. Accused of wrongdoing, we respond, "Who me?" "I didn't do it," "It's only a game," "Well, you asked for it," or "I didn't mean to."

But let's be honest. We are responsible. As human beings with a free will we have choices, and nobody makes them for us. While we are not necessarily the cause of all that happens in our lives, we are responsible for what we make of what happens. As Scripture says, "You, my brothers and sisters, were called to be free. But do not use your freedom to indulge the flesh; rather, serve one another humbly in love" (Gal. 5:13).

Dr. M. Scott Peck, in his bestselling *The Road Less Traveled*, writes about the tendency unhealthy people have to give their free will away. "Sooner or later, if they are to be healed, they must learn that the entirety of one's adult life is a series of personal choices, decisions. If they can accept this totally, then they become free people. To the extent they do not accept this, they will forever feel themselves victims."

Don't let your marriage become a blame game. Don't lay the blame on your church, your parents, your schooling, your income, your siblings, your friends, your government, or anything else. Take responsibility for your feelings and your actions, and watch your marriage mature.

FROM GOD'S WORD

Carry each other's burdens, and in this way you will fulfill the law of
Christ. If anyone thinks they are something when they are not, they
deceive themselves. Each one should test their own actions. Then
they can take pride in themselves alone, without comparing themselves to someone else, for each one should carry their own load.

GALATIANS 6:2–5

YOUR TURN

- The Bible emphasizes personal responsibility and free will.
  Why do you think this is part of the gospel message?
- Have you noticed society's tendency toward victimhood?
  Why do you think so many people are quick to blame others?
- Give an example of a time when you decided to rise
  above your negative circumstances. How did you adjust to
  something that was beyond your control? What allowed
  you to have a positive attitude?
- How does your partner demonstrate personal responsibility?
  What mature choices have you seen him or her make?
- In practical terms, what can you and your partner do to
  foster a blame-free relationship?

SOUL TO SOUL

To deepen your spiritual intimacy this next week, make note of:

- What you gained from this session together.
- A pressure point in your partner's upcoming week you
  will pray about.
- A concrete kindness you can offer your partner this week.

PRAYER

Dear God, help us to stay on the sidelines when others are playing the blame game. We strive to be responsible, to be accountable, and to be honest. Since these goals are hard to achieve consistently, we need your special help this week and in the weeks to come. Amen.

Real-Life Soul Mates

Spiritual growth isn't easy. Spiritual growth as a couple is even more difficult. Trisha and I have spent more than twenty years in ministry. We are supposed to be professionals at spiritual growth. Despite our Bible college education, spiritual growth in our marriage was anemic for many years.

One of the reasons we struggled in this area is that we looked at spiritual disciplines as a box we needed to fit into rather than a relationship to be developed. Most of the time we felt guilty for not praying or not reading the Bible or not journaling. Instead, we should have been pursuing intimacy with God and each other.

A few years ago, we made some changes in our marriage that drastically increased the intimacy we feel with one another and the intimacy we experience in our relationship with God. Here are a few shifts we've made that have helped us.

First, we recognize that marriage is physical and marriage is emotional but more than anything else, marriage is spiritual. We quit treating each other as enemies and instead started fighting the spiritual enemy in our marriage. Now we assume the best of each other and fight the spiritual battle together.

Second, we got serious about prayer. When you choose to share the intimacy of prayer with your spouse, an intimacy is birthed in your marriage that is rich and deep. Here is the key when it comes to prayer: pray what's in your heart, not what you think should be in your heart. Trying to be perfect in prayer doesn't impress God; it only limits the amount of intimacy you can experience with him. When you choose to be vulnerable in prayer with your spouse, your marriage grows in intimacy.

Finally, we give grace freely in our marriage. What we realized is that so much of our spiritual development as a couple was being held back by built-up resentment toward one another. Jesus said in essence, "He who has been forgiven of much, loves much" (see Luke 7:47). Only when we realize our own need for grace will we be truly able to love our spouse with the grace-giving love of Jesus. You can read the Bible every day, pray every hour, and fast every week, but if you are holding on to bitterness, you won't grow intimacy in your marriage relationship.

What God desires for us is not behavior modification but heart transformation. As we pursue God and pursue each other, we stop trying to change our spouse into the person we want them to be and free them to be transformed into the spouse that God created them to be.

Justin and Trisha Davis

YOU'RE NOT THE BOSS OF ME!

Chaim Potok's novel *The Chosen* tells the story of a young boy born to a Hasidic rabbi. As the boy matures, his father recognizes that his child is especially clever and gifted, if not already a little arrogant and impatient. Knowing that his boy was likely to become the rabbi of his people, the father makes a mysterious and difficult decision not to speak to the boy. He raises the boy in a house without the comfort of a speaking relationship. As the story draws to a close, Potok reveals that the father has chosen this unconventional path of parenthood with the boy because he wanted to create in him the capacity for understanding and compassion. He wanted him to minister from a heart that knows pain and can feel the pain of others. The father feared that his son's analytic brilliance and arrogance would rob him of the capacity to love.

The father in Potok's novel intuitively understood how keen analytic abilities, unsoftened by emotional tenderness, lead to manipulation rather than ministry, how they lead to control rather than compassion.

You may not agree with this rabbi's methods, but it is difficult to dispute his insight. When your head is not linked to your heart, real love is difficult to muster—especially in marriage. The result is a spouse we sometimes call "The Controller."

Controllers, analytic by nature, typically use two powerful tools in gaining and maintaining control in their marriage. The first is fear. Controllers have refined the technique of "winning through intimidation." They have a hawklike eye for their partner's weakness, and their partner knows it. Without so much as a peep, the Controller can fire fear and anxiety into his or her mate like Rambo fires a machine gun.

The second tool of control is guilt. A Controlling husband can make his wife feel guilty for not having supper on the table at exactly six o'clock. A Controlling wife can maneuver her husband into performing tasks for which she is actually responsible by laying on a sense of obligation and guilt. Controllers needle the conscience of their partner to provoke them to do what the Controllers want done.

The disciple Peter, in his own bungling way, was a Controller. He kept trying to tell Jesus what to do and what to say, to the point where Jesus rebuked him sharply: "Get behind me, Satan! You are a stumbling block to me; you do not have in mind the concerns of God, but merely human concerns" (Matt. 16:23). Finally, humbled by his denial of Jesus, Peter became an effective leader of the new church, even admitting his fault when Paul confronted him for forcing Gentiles to follow Jewish laws (Gal. 2:11–14).

Well, maybe you are lucky. Perhaps neither of you has controlling tendencies, but I (Les) do. I'm sometimes bossy with Leslie and feel compelled to give her unnecessary advice. Over the years, however, I've gotten better. Like Peter, I am willing to admit my faults. How about you?

FROM GOD'S WORD

You, then, why do you judge your brother or sister? Or why do you treat them with contempt? For we will all stand before God's judgment seat. It is written:

"'As surely as I live,' says the Lord,
'Every knee will bow before me;
every tongue will acknowledge God.'"

So then, each of us will give an account of ourselves to God. Therefore let us stop passing judgment on one another. Instead, make up your mind not to put any stumbling block or obstacle in the way of a brother or sister.

Romans 14:10–13

YOUR TURN

- How can you work together to keep the destructive influence of guilt and fear from entering into your marriage?
- Give an example of a time when you received compassion and understanding from your partner.
- Why do you think Christ so strongly admonishes us not to pass judgment on each other (see Luke 6:37)?
- Give an example of how you have been motivated to do something for your mate because you felt guilty.
- What is one step you can take together as a couple that will decrease controlling maneuvers in your relationship?

SOUL TO SOUL

To deepen your spiritual intimacy this next week, make note of:

- What you gained from this session together.
- A pressure point in your partner's upcoming week you will pray about.
- A concrete kindness you can offer your partner this week.

PRAYER

Dear God, we long for a love that is free from fear and guilt. Help us to work on relinquishing our controlling tendencies and exchange them for genuine love that works in the situations of our lives. May we feel the pain but multiply the joys of each other as our marriage moves forward for another week. Amen.

Real-Life Soul Mates

Years ago, I wish someone would have done what Les and Leslie Parrott are doing through this devotional book. We could have learned so much! Our first year of marriage was our most difficult. But when we started taking steps to grow spiritually and began to understand the value of our personality differences, our marriage deepened. We discovered a routine in each season of our marriage to cultivate spiritual intimacy. Different methods worked at different times.

Perhaps the one constant that has helped us grow closer as a couple has been prayer. Beth and I pray together each night in bed. We started doing this early on in our marriage. Usually just one of us prays each night. And yes, there have been times when one has fallen asleep during the other's prayer. A few times, I have even fallen asleep during *my own* prayer.

The longer we've been married, prayer has become more of a conversation with each of us "interrupting" and joining in at times. Early on, I think we were self-conscious about the way our prayers sounded. If you feel the same, we can tell you that those petty concerns will quickly disappear when you both take the risk and go for it. Thanking God and sharing your fears or concerns for the upcoming day is a great way to close out each evening. Strangely, you'll also find that prayer fosters sexual intimacy, too.

We are thankful that years ago we were encouraged to make going to bed at the same time a high priority. This principle has been extremely rewarding, and we have stuck with it about 95 percent of the time. That may mean sacrificing a TV show or cutting back on social media for the sake of that intimacy. And even when we don't actually get to bed at the same time, we still pray together before one of us returns to whatever the late-night project (or major sporting event!) happens to be.

Another way we have been able to draw closer is by hosting a Bible study for young married couples in our home in the spring and fall. This allows my wife's gift of hospitality and my gift of teaching to be utilized together, as a team. Pouring into other people strengthens and deepens your own relationship.

We also enjoy having parties and get-togethers for people who are sometimes overlooked. We both like to encourage people and make them feel special. We have derived fulfillment from that through the years, even in our first home that was a mere nine hundred square feet.

God is faithful! In every season he provides us new opportunities for our marriage to deepen.

Dave and Beth Stone

Session Thirty-Four

SEX, SEX, SEX ...
ENOUGH ALREADY!

In the film *Annie Hall*, Woody Allen and Diane Keaton are shown split-screen as each talks to an analyst about their sexual relationship. When the analyst asks how often they have sex, he answers, "Hardly ever, maybe three times a week," while she describes it as, "Constantly, three times a week."

How is it that a husband and wife can view sex so differently? One reason is that they are socialized in different ways about sexuality and marriage. Men tend to see sex as a pleasurable physical activity, while women see it as a sign of emotional commitment. These separate meanings can become the source of much miscommunication and misunderstanding in marriage. Consider the following comments made by a wife and husband after three or four years of marriage:

Wife: He keeps saying he wants to make love, but it doesn't feel like love to me. Sometimes I feel bad that I feel that way, but I just can't help it.

Husband: I don't understand. She says it doesn't feel like love. What does that mean, anyway? What does she think love is? I want to have sex with her because I love her!

In this marriage, as in many others, the husband sees himself as showing his love to his wife by engaging her in sexual activity. The wife, on the other hand, sees sexual activity as something that should evolve out of verbal expressions of affection and love. Like a scene from a Woody Allen movie that cuts too close to home, this couple bickers continually about how frequently they have sex.

Of course, the question about how much lovemaking is enough is not a matter of counting the number of times per week that a Christian couple may decently have sex. There is no prescription, no magic number. For partners who are dedicated to the personal life of each other, the question of frequency will be answered in terms of concern for the needs and desires of the other person.

Our friend and former professor, Lewis Smedes, says this in his book *Sex for Christians*: "The moral issue is never 'how much' sex but whether physical sex is being integrated into a pattern of personal dedication. What happens 'between the times' is more important than how many times."

Spouses need to be realistic about their sex life and willing to accommodate each other's desires. Granted, not every sexual experience is going to be equally satisfying and fulfilling for both partners. But if you rejoice in the husband or wife of your youth, you will be captivated by each other's love (see Prov. 5:18–20).

FROM GOD'S WORD

I belong to my beloved, and his desire is for me. Come, my beloved, let us go to the countryside, let us spend the night in the villages. Let us go early to the vineyards to see if the vines have budded, if their blossoms have opened, and if the pomegranates are in bloom—there I will give you my love.

Song of Songs 7:10–12

YOUR TURN

- Do you identify with the scenario in the opening paragraph of this session? Why or why not?
- What causes tension in your sexual relations? What, if anything, do you disagree about and why?
- Give an example of an intimate encounter with your partner that brought you deep emotional fulfillment. What made it that way for you?
- Discuss how your sexuality can be woven into a pattern of personal dedication as a couple. What concrete steps can each of you take toward this goal?
- How can you infuse your sexual intimacy with more physical pleasure?

SOUL TO SOUL

To deepen your spiritual intimacy this next week, make note of:

- What you gained from this session together.
- A pressure point in your partner's upcoming week you will pray about.
- A concrete kindness you can offer your partner this week.

PRAYER

Almighty God, allow us to experience the fullness of rejoicing in each other's love. Uphold us as we seek to weave sexual intimacy into a pattern of personal dedication to one another. Help us as a couple to satisfy the desires of our hearts. In the name of Christ, amen.

Real-Life Soul Mates

Jeanette and I got married young, and we didn't really know what we were doing at first. We got a lot of advice from older couples, some of which we welcomed and some of which just seemed odd and out of place, but which we took anyway, because we knew the couples giving it to us at least meant well.

One piece of advice we got that we really took to heart had to do with the number *one*. We determined to put that number to use in our relationship, so that we could truly become one. Here's how it worked. We agreed to dedicate time together in the following ways:

- One hour every day
- One night every week
- One weekend every month
- One week every year

Now, of course, we spend a lot of time together outside those parameters, but we decided we needed to be intentional about budgeting this kind of time, especially once we started having kids and work/ministry obligations and soccer practices and all the other things that eventually steal all your time from you.

But in the midst of all that, we've stuck to the *one*.

It hasn't always been easy. Sometimes we've had to really work hard to find that hour together every night. We haven't always been able to afford the weeklong vacation, whether because of the money or the time away. But we've stretched and saved and sorted things out to make our *one* happen.

And what do we do during our one? Sometimes we talk about important things like God or everyday things like grocery lists. We have sex! Yes, I said it. We have realized how important sex is in our relationship and the intimacy that it builds, so we have worked to make that a priority as well. We don't follow a schedule or itinerary—we just do all we can to relate to one another, learn from (and about!) one another, and give to one another.

We want to become one so that we can serve the One. And so we work for the One. And I can honestly say that, when it comes to marriage, we've won.

Craig and Jeanette Gross

PAY NOW, PLAY LATER

We have always had separate closets. And it's a good thing. Mine is a total wreck. Les's closet, however, looks like a page from *Architectural Digest*. He has a place for everything and takes the time to put things where they belong. I, on the other hand, put things wherever it is convenient . . . the back of a chair, the floor. You get the picture.

Well, Les has never been too pushy as a neatnik, but his self-discipline has rubbed off. Not that my clothes routinely make it onto cedar hangers, but I have come to appreciate a particular quality of the highly organized: delayed gratification. It's the ability to patiently put off immediate rewards in order to enjoy greater benefits later on.

Saving money is a prime example. Two years into our marriage, the only vehicle we had, a gray Ford pickup truck, was on its last legs. *Yippee!* I thought to myself. I was ready to cruise the car lots and bring home a new sporty model. "We could probably get a new car for three hundred dollars a month," I told Les.

He had another idea: "Don't you think we'd be better off to avoid the interest of a loan and pay cash for a car?" The thought had never occurred to me. But we began to talk about how we could cut back on this and that, and we soon came up with a plan to delay our immediate desires and enjoy the freedom of a new car debt-free. We have paid cash for every car we've had since.

But delayed gratification does not just apply to saving money. It is a principle that applies to living. M. Scott Peck, in his bestselling book *The Road Less Traveled*, states: "Delaying gratification is a process of scheduling the pain and pleasure of life in such a way as to enhance the pleasure by meeting and experiencing the pain first and getting it over with. It is the only decent way to live." Scheduling the easy and the hard applies to everything from cleaning the house to earning an education.

The key to delayed gratification is patience. It's a virtue endorsed by Scripture. Patience, for example, is a fruit of the Spirit (Gal. 5:22). As Paul prayed for Christians he often asked God to give them patience (Col. 1:11). Timothy was commended by Paul for his patience (2 Tim. 3:10). And the book of Hebrews characterizes the Christian life as an exercise in patience (12:1–3). But the ultimate example of delayed gratification and patience is Christ (see 2 Peter 3:9, 15). When the devil tempted him with the splendor of "all the kingdoms of the world," Jesus refused, knowing that he would ultimately enter the kingdom of God (Matt. 4:1–11).

Putting our immediate gratification temporarily in abeyance can strengthen the marriage bonds. Couples who do not develop the capacity for delayed gratification become impulsive and are soon swayed by every whim of the moment. But couples who forgo some instant pleasures to cultivate the discipline of delaying their gratification reap meaningful and fulfilling rewards. "Patience," as a German proverb says, "is a bitter plant, but it bears sweet fruit."

FROM GOD'S WORD

Therefore, since we are surrounded by such a great cloud of witnesses, let us throw off everything that hinders and the sin that so easily entangles. And let us run with perseverance the race marked out for us, fixing our eyes on Jesus, the pioneer and perfecter of faith. For the joy set before him he endured the cross, scorning its shame, and sat down at the right hand of the throne of God. Consider him who endured such opposition from sinners, so that you will not grow weary and lose heart.

HEBREWS 12:1–3

YOUR TURN

- Discuss how each of you practices the art of delaying your gratification. Does it come easier to one of you than it does the other?
- Give an example of how you personally have patiently practiced delayed gratification.
- How do patience and delayed gratification relate to your spiritual journey with Christ?
- Name one or two areas in your lives that could benefit from the discipline of delayed gratification. How could you as a couple practice it?
- How could practicing delayed gratification buoy your marriage?

SOUL TO SOUL

To deepen your spiritual intimacy this next week, make note of:

- What you gained from this session together.
- A pressure point in your partner's upcoming week you will pray about.
- A concrete kindness you can offer your partner this week.

PRAYER

Gracious God, we thank you for patience, one of the fruits of your Spirit. Help us to encourage its growth and development in our marriage. We want to make choices based on wisdom instead of ease. Reveal to us the rewards that come in delaying our gratification for better results. Amen.

Real-Life Soul Mates

So, we're on our honeymoon. Third night, somewhere in the rolling hills of Virginia. Bill is taking a shower, I'm channel surfing. By the time he reappears, freshly shaved and wrapped in a towel, I'm deeply engrossed in a Billy Graham sermon on TV. Yes, really.

Bill joins me at the end of the bed. "Not exactly how I pictured spending our honeymoon," he teases me. Two minutes later, he's watching as intently as I am. We start discussing effective ways to share the gospel, and we end up praying about how we might serve the Lord in the months and years to come.

Not to worry, we soon returned to our regularly scheduled program—newlywed shenanigans—but that scene set the tone for our married life. Hardly a day goes by without some spontaneous exchange of spiritual ideas and beliefs, firmly rooted in Scripture. Scheduling daily devotions together just isn't our thing (sorry!), but regular, meaningful conversations about God and his Word? Absolutely.

I didn't marry until I was almost thirty-two, so I had plenty of time to consider what kind of guy would make a great husband. Tall, dark, and handsome weren't even on the list. My top five? Trustworthy, joyful, confident, flexible, and, above all, a man after God's own heart. (The fact that he's tall, *silver*, and handsome is a bonus!)

Bill, nearly thirty-four when we married, had just two things on his list: a woman who shared his core values and would be an equal partner intellectually and spiritually. Those are the qualities that go the distance, that aren't dependent on how good we look, how much we have in our bank account, or how happy we're feeling at the moment.

We also pray together a crazy number of times a day. Pass an accident on the road? We pray. See a post on social media from a hurting friend? We pray. Get a phone call from Bill's aging father? We pray. Sit down to a meal, even in a restaurant? We pray, with heads bowed and hands clasped. God's call to "pray continually" (1 Thess. 5:17) is something we take to heart.

Spiritual intimacy may not be a phrase we often use around the house, but it's a truth we live out daily. I am more in love with Bill than the day we said "I do" because of all the ways he's demonstrated his love for God by loving me. My goal? To do the same and honor our vows—not "until death do us part," but forever.

Bill and Liz Curtis Higgs

HOW TO BE A WISE GUY (AND GAL)

Falling in love is a dizzying experience. Once the spark of attraction catches flame, love quickly turns into a raging fire of unreasoned passion. Engulfed by its heat, couples sometimes sacrifice all sound judgment in the interest of bonding their relationship. The Song of Songs says, "Many waters cannot quench love; rivers cannot sweep it away" (8:7). Love, by its very nature, is extravagant.

We once read about a man who hired a helicopter to drop 2,500 carnations and 10,000 love letters on the lawn of a woman he loved. Apparently the woman failed to share this man's affection and had him charged with littering. She told reporters, "He had lost his mind."

Love really can cause some people to lose their heads. They become "crazy in love." They become compelled by the emotional force of love and forsake their analytical ability. It's a common danger. If we let it, passion can override our capacity to think clearly. That is why Scripture urges us to "be very careful, then, how you live—not as unwise, but as wise" (Eph. 5:15).

Have you thought much about wisdom—the ability to reason with insight? You should. It is essential to the success of your marriage. Sure, the emotional side of love is vital, and you will need to stoke the fires of passion over the years, but don't neglect the cool calm of wisdom.

Wisdom is not about saying wise words or doing wise deeds. It is concerned with being, not doing. So how do you cultivate wisdom in marriage? Or, as Job asked, "Where can wisdom be found? Where does understanding dwell?" (28:12). The writer of Proverbs compared searching for wisdom to mining and said, "If you look for it as for silver and search for it as for hidden treasure, then you will understand" (2:4–5).

After a decade of marriage we are still on an expedition for more wisdom. Daily we seek to avoid being unwise, and we have discovered two tools that are essential in our pursuit.

First of all, we have learned that wisdom only comes when we are humble. As Socrates said, "The wisest man is he who knows his own ignorance." Without humility marriage partners fall victim to pride, and "when pride comes, then comes disgrace, but with humility comes wisdom" (Prov. 11:2). So be humble enough to ask for help. Learn how to ask a good question. According to Francis Bacon, "A prudent question is one-half of wisdom."

The second tool for mining wisdom in marriage stems from the first—ask God to share his wisdom with you (see James 1:5). Human wisdom on its own is inadequate (see 1 Cor. 1:19; 1:21; 3:18–19). We need the wisdom that comes from God, for "the fear of the Lord is the beginning of wisdom" (Ps. 111:10; see also Prov. 9:10; Matt. 12:42; 13:54; Acts 6:3).

So enjoy the dizzying emotions of love for your partner, but never neglect the importance of wisdom in marriage. It is a shared pursuit for soul mates, and it will bless your union.

FROM GOD'S WORD

Blessed are those who find wisdom, those who gain understanding, for she is more profitable than silver and yields better returns than gold. She is more precious than rubies; nothing you desire can compare with her. Long life is in her right hand; in her left hand are riches and honor. Her ways are pleasant ways, and all her paths are peace. She is a tree of life to those who take hold of her; those who hold her fast will be blessed.

PROVERBS 3:13–18

YOUR TURN

- Scripture points to the fact that wisdom is more about who you are as a person than it is about what you say or do. What do you make of this?
- Was there a time in your relationship when the emotions of love overruled sound judgment? What can you learn from that experience?
- Give an example of a time when you humbled yourself to ask for help. How did it increase your wisdom?
- Is it a struggle for you to ask for help? How about your partner? Does it prevent either one of you from becoming "wise"?
- In what areas do you find that your spouse is especially wise? How did he or she develop that wisdom?

SOUL TO SOUL

To deepen your spiritual intimacy this next week, make note of:

- What you gained from this session together.
- A pressure point in your partner's upcoming week you will pray about.
- A concrete kindness you can offer your partner this week.

PRAYER

Gracious God, you have promised to give wisdom generously to all who ask. And now we are asking. Fill us with wisdom as we invest our time, talents, and resources in our shared future. Build us up into people of humility who are quick to learn and quick to seek your counsel. Amen.

Real-Life Soul Mates

We first met in Germany, where Tammy's family served as missionaries, and where we became engaged in a little café in Hamburg a short time later. Knowing Chris was heading into full-time ministry as a pastor and church planter, we both knew our ability to love each other had to be firmly rooted in our love for Christ.

Now almost thirty years later, we remain completely convinced that our ability to love, to forgive, and to remain faithful to one another results directly from our love relationship with Jesus. The Bible says, "We love because he first loved us" (1 John 4:19). Experiencing God's love individually gives us the capacity to love each other as husband and wife and to accept our differences.

Which hasn't always been easy, since we could not be more opposite in many ways. When one of us is hot, the other's freezing. When one of us wants to discipline the kids, the other wants to show mercy. When one wants to watch *Dumb and Dumber* (you can probably guess which one), the other wants to see *Pride and Prejudice*.

The ways we're each called to serve in ministry is also very different. As a senior pastor and a committed church planter, Chris preaches to thousands of people each week, leads conferences, and travels frequently.

Tammy, on the other hand, feels her primary calling is to be a wife and mom. She has no desire to be in the spotlight and feels called to minister more personally to those around her.

We quickly realized our differences could either irritate us or entertain us, either drive us apart or make us better as a team. Since we're both committed to God first, we learned to accept our differences and enjoy them. We regularly pray together, read the Bible together, and discuss what God is showing us so that we can then serve others in the different ways God has called each of us.

Our spiritual intimacy grows when we celebrate our differences, knowing we're designed to complement—not compete with—one another.

Chris and Tammy Hodges

THE ROLE OF OPTIMISM IN MARRIAGE

Ron and Cindy came to us after three years of marriage because they were calling it quits. We were their last-ditch effort to save a sinking marriage. Soon into our first counseling session we saw just why this young couple was already throwing in the towel. They were pessimists, defeated, disappointed, and depressed. They never expected their marriage to get any better. All they could see were problems, no solutions. So they gave up hope.

Nothing is more deadly to marriage than negativism, especially in its most alluring form of pessimism. In fact, if couples could be given a vaccine against pessimistic thinking, we would see the divorce rate drop. In a sense, you can protect your marriage against a pessimistic virus. All it takes is a good shot of optimism.

No psychologist has helped us understand optimism more than Dr. Martin Seligman at the University of Pennsylvania. As a twenty-one-year-old graduate student fresh out of college, he observed an experiment that sent him on a lifelong quest to find out why some people seek opportunity while others give up.

In the experiment Dr. Seligman observed, dogs were subjected to a minor shock, which they could avoid by jumping over a low wall separating two sides of a shuttle box. Most dogs learned this task easily. But other dogs just lay down whimpering. They had no will to try. When Seligman investigated the dogs who had given up, he found they had been used in a prior experiment in which they received shocks no matter what they did. These dogs had "learned" helplessness. Because they had been given shocks regardless of whether they struggled or jumped or barked or did nothing, they learned that nothing they did mattered. So why try?

Like Seligman's dogs, marriages can fall victim to learned helplessness. When a couple begins to see every problem as interminable, or when they believe one problem will ruin everything, they quit trying. They raise the white flag and surrender to problems they could otherwise beat. *You and I are never going to be any different*, they reason, *so why try?*

Someone defined a pessimist as one who feels bad when he feels good for fear he'll feel worse when he feels better. Pessimists have simply made negative thinking a habit, a way of life. Optimists, on the other hand, are undaunted by defeat. When they are confronted with the inevitable hard knocks of life, they immediately look for solutions. They see defeat as temporary.

The Bible has a different word for optimism—*hope*. In the New Testament, the word *hope* appears more than eighty times, and it usually refers to Christ, who is the hope of this world (see Titus 2:13; 1 Peter 1:3). Colossians 1:5 tells us that love springs from hope. Another New Testament writer called hope "an anchor for the soul, firm and secure" (Heb. 6:19), and Paul said it "does not put us to shame" (Rom. 5:5). He also alluded to hope as being an attitude of optimism when he urged the Thessalonians to put on "hope . . . as a helmet" (1 Thess. 5:8). Hope protects our head. It is an attitude that safeguards optimism and protects a marriage.

FROM GOD'S WORD

For in this hope we were saved. But hope that is seen is no hope
at all. Who hopes for what they already have? But if we hope for
what we do not yet have, we wait for it patiently.

ROMANS 8:24–25

YOUR TURN

- Why do you think hope is talked about so often in
  Scripture?
- Give an example of a time when you saw your partner
  demonstrate hope and optimism.
- Have you ever fallen victim to learned helplessness and
  given up hope? What did you do to overcome it?
- Talk about the home you grew up in. Was it basically
  optimistic or pessimistic? What can each of you learn
  about being optimists from your families?
- Is there something right now in your life that could be
  given a boost with a shot of optimism? How can you help
  each other cultivate this virtue?

SOUL TO SOUL

To deepen your spiritual intimacy this next week, make note of:

- What you gained from this session together.
- A pressure point in your partner's upcoming week you
  will pray about.
- A concrete kindness you can offer your partner this week.

PRAYER

To you, O Lord, we lift up our souls because we trust in you. We proclaim confidently that our hope is in you. In the midst of our discouragements help us to take refuge, together, in our ultimate Hope. Infuse our marriage relationship with a continuing attitude of optimism. Amen.

Real-Life Soul Mates

We have been married thirty-five years, practiced medicine together for twenty-five years, and raised four children. Over the years, friends have asked, "How do you work together and have a good marriage?" I have always found this question peculiar, and both of us answer the same, "Practicing medicine together is easy, but raising four children together—that's hard!"

The same is true for spiritual intimacy for us. We share a deep spiritual intimacy currently, but it took years to develop. We arrived there by trial and error. As enthusiastic believers in our early thirties, we went to Bible studies with other couples and really enjoyed those. Then we tried praying together regularly, but that was more difficult in the early years because our schedules were different and we had small children. Finding time to be alone for even fifteen minutes was a frustrating challenge. When he was ready to pray, I was exhausted, and when I was ready, he wasn't around.

As the kids grew older, we read Scripture together and found this difficult too. We found the time, but believe it or not, we often disagreed (in small ways) on what the Scriptures meant. We would become frustrated with one another and realized that we needed a new plan.

We are both committed to serving the poor, so we started working at a local soup kitchen once per month. We've done this for about twenty years now and love working side-by-side for people in Jesus' name. We ask one another what we need to pray for and we pray diligently for one another. We also talk about God's will in our lives and consult one another regularly about the work we do, schedules we keep, and money we spend, and we ask each other if we are in the center of God's will. We are completely honest with one another and really listen to one another's advice.

Finally, we talk about Jesus a lot to one another. In fact, we show one another how he is working and what he did for us during the day, and we regularly express to each other our love and gratitude for him. This is really the heart of how we experience spiritual intimacy. It is a bit unusual because the normal habits of studying Scripture together and praying with one another regularly don't work consistently for us.

I guess we just keep it kind of simple. We love Jesus with all our hearts and help one another do the same. And the bonus to this is that our marriage has taken on a wonderful depth, and we feel Jesus living between the two of us.

Walt and Meg Meeker

Session Thirty-Eight

THE VALUE OF TENDER TOUCH

In May 1985, Brigitte Gerney was trapped for six hours beneath a thirty-five-ton collapsed construction crane in New York City. Throughout her ordeal, she held the hand of officer Paul Ragonese, who stayed by her side as heavy machinery moved the tons of twisted steel from her crushed legs. A stranger's touch gave her hope and the will to live.

Touch is one of the most powerful communication tools.

From a mother's cradling embrace to a friend's comforting hug or a marriage partner's caress, touch has the special power to send messages of union and communion. Even a momentary and seemingly incidental touch on your partner's shoulder or hand can strengthen the marital bond by conveying affirmation, comfort, and security.

Both the toucher and the one being touched receive emotional and physiological benefits. Stacks of research, for example, have shown that a gentle touch or hug can cause a speeding heart to quiet, soaring blood pressure to drop, and severe pain to ease. A study at UCLA estimated that if some "type-A driven" men would hug their wives several times each day, it would increase their life span by almost two years, not to mention the way it would improve their marriages. That same study reported that eight to ten meaningful touches each day help us maintain emotional and physical health.

Scripture shows the value of touch as it conveys a blessing (see Gen. 27:26; Gen. 48:9–14). In the Old Testament, the people laid their hands on the Levites to demonstrate that they were setting them apart for their priestly duties (Num. 8:10). Moses laid his hands on Joshua to symbolize that he was giving Joshua authority over the people (Num. 27:18). And Jesus, of course, was a master of communicating love through touch: "And he took the children in his arms, placed his hands on them and blessed them" (Mark 10:16).

So consider the value of meaningful touch to your marriage. If a stranger's touch meant life to Brigitte Gerney, think of what a meaningful touch from you can do for your partner.

FROM GOD'S WORD

Just then a woman who had been subject to bleeding for twelve years came up behind him and touched the edge of his cloak. She said to herself, "If I only touch his cloak, I will be healed." Jesus turned and saw her. "Take heart, daughter," he said, "your faith has healed you." And the woman was healed at that moment.

MATTHEW 9:20–22

[Jesus] reached out his hand and touched the man. . . . Immediately the leprosy left him and he was cleansed.

MARK 1:41–42

YOUR TURN

- Why do you think Christ was so attuned to personal touch?

- Give an example of how you benefited from a recent touch from your partner.
- When do you most often want to be touched by your partner and in what ways?
- Do you feel differently about touching in public versus touching in private?
- What is the one thing you would like your partner to understand about you and touching?

SOUL TO SOUL

To deepen your spiritual intimacy this next week, make note of:

- What you gained from this session together.
- A pressure point in your partner's upcoming week you will pray about.
- A concrete kindness you can offer your partner this week.

PRAYER

Gracious God, we thank you for the meaning—even the healing—of one human being reaching out to touch another person. Your touch gives us hope and motivation to reach out our healing arms to one another. We thank you for the precious gift of a gentle caress. Help us to practice the ministry of meaningful touch with each other this week. Amen.

Real-Life Soul Mates

When Shirley and I were married at age nineteen in Nashville, Mack Craig gave us a Bible with our married names on it. It's the only wedding gift that has stayed with us through the years. We've read it together, we've prayed together, and we've always been faithful in church attendance and activity.

And still we almost "came unglued."

The entertainment business takes a terrible toll on marriages. The stress and temptations tore at the very underpinnings of our marriage, and for two years we thought it was over. But one day, walking past the piano in our living room, I focused on a picture of Shirley that I'd seen countless times before. This time it transfixed me. It was a picture of her at the age of three, with her arms around her father, Red Foley, and the adoring, needful, poignant expression of that little girl seared itself into my heart. I realized that she was still that little girl. Oh, she was now in her thirties with four kids, and a wonderful wife and mother. I was used to seeing her as a grown woman, with some of the wounds and resulting defenses right at the surface. Her dad had recently gone to be with the Lord, and I knew that little girl still needed a man to protect, love, and nurture her.

Suddenly, I wanted to be that man. I shared that with her, and we shared some tears. The next Father's Day, she gave me a framed picture of her as a little girl, and on the back she wrote: "Take care of this little girl—she needs you."

It's been twenty-five years or more now, and I pray and worship with that little girl, my grown-up wife, all the time. We're growing older, but we're still kids to each other—and somehow, kids can just love God and each other better than grown-ups. What was it that Jesus said? "Unless you change and become like little children, you will never enter into the kingdom of heaven" (Matt. 18:2).

Pat and Shirley Boone

NO ONE NEEDS TO BE A FOOL

A young bride, getting settled into the routine of married life, cooked a ham for her new husband. Before putting it in the pan, she cut off both ends. When her husband asked her why she did that, she replied that her mother had always done it that way. At a later date, when they were having a baked ham dinner at her mother's home, the young husband asked his mother-in-law, casually, why she cut off both ends of the ham. The mother shrugged and said she really didn't know, except that her mother had always done it that way. Finally, he asked the grandmother why she always cut off the ends the ham before she baked it. The grandmother looked at him suspiciously, replying, "Because my baking dish was too small!"

Sometimes, without even knowing it, we do silly things. And while needlessly baking a sawed-off ham has no serious effects, some blunders can lead to downright foolish results. Is *foolish* too strong a word? Probably not. "A fool," said William Thackeray, "can no more see his own folly than he can see his ears."

We know a couple, married six years, who didn't make it. They made some foolish choices and never had a clue as to how they were blowing their marriage apart. Everything started out

189

fine. In fact it was more than fine. They came from good homes and were raised in the church. They had more advantages for a successful marriage than most. But somewhere along the line they began to take their heritage and their relationship with God for granted. Slowly, they gravitated away from their values and made compromises with their faith. His business involved traveling, and their frequent separations became ripe for foolish decisions. It was then only a matter of time before the relationship folded.

We can never totally escape silly blunders; that's what makes life interesting. But no one needs to be a fool. For according to Scripture there is really only one thing that can make anyone a fool—missing out on God's will. Paul says, "Do not be foolish, but understand what the Lord's will is" (Eph. 5:17).

Every couple needs the wisdom that comes in seeking God's will for their relationship. Without God's direction, foolish decisions are bound to happen and then a string of side effects appears. The Bible says that a fool is quick to quarrel (Prov. 20:3), scorns wisdom (Prov. 23:9), repeats mistakes again and again (Prov. 26:11), has no peace (Prov. 29:9), can't control his anger (Prov. 29:11), and is cocky (Prov. 30:32). Can you imagine trying to live with the person who is not seeking the Lord's will? "Better to meet a bear robbed of her cubs," says Proverbs, "than a fool bent on folly" (17:12).

FROM GOD'S WORD

Be very careful, then, how you live—not as unwise but as wise, making the most of every opportunity, because the days are evil. Therefore do not be foolish, but understand what the Lord's will is. Do not get drunk on wine, which leads to debauchery. Instead, be filled with the Spirit.

EPHESIANS 5:15–18

YOUR TURN

- How have you sought God's will in your life and what difference has it made?
- Wise decisions take time. What goes into your decision making process as a couple?
- Many things can lead to foolish choices. Chief among them is anger. Has anger ever led you to a foolish choice? How?
- If you were to be as specific as possible, what do you think God's will for your marriage is this week?
- In practical terms, what can you and your partner do to protect your marriage against foolish choices?

SOUL TO SOUL

To deepen your spiritual intimacy this next week, make note of:

- What you gained from this session together.
- A pressure point in your partner's upcoming week you will pray about.
- A concrete kindness you can offer your partner this week.

PRAYER

Almighty God, we recognize the need for good judgment in all we do. Save us from the misjudgments that come in being hasty or superficial. Teach us to depend on the wisdom of people we trust. And most of all, teach us to hear your still, small voice, which is so easily drowned out by the racket of everyday living. Amen.

Real-Life Soul Mates

Spiritual intimacy. The very words hang heavy with an aura of the ethereal, unattainable, and unreachable.

Early in our marriage we decided we weren't going to "program" spiritual intimacy into our lives, thus setting ourselves up for failure. Because of work, school, and small children, the set-time spiritual schedule was more of a burden than a blessing.

Instead, we chose to view spiritual intimacy as a natural, spontaneous, and foundational means of relating to each other. Spiritual intimacy is not something we do: it literally defines who we are as a couple. However, we have made some intentional decisions to develop our spiritual relationship. We make a conscious effort to share some spiritual question as it relates to a family problem, a book we've been reading, a sermon in the making, a Bible study lesson, or even political issues. The discussions may take place on the phone, over a meal, walking, riding in the car, in bed, or even in the church foyer between services. The point is, not a day passes when we don't connect as a couple with the bigger spiritual picture of life.

The days have now stretched into more than forty years of marriage. Spiritual intimacy is as attainable, practical, and natural to us as developing a family budget.

We can think of no greater marital legacy than to be known as spiritual intimates.

Gary and Jorie Gulbranson

Session Forty

HAVING THE TITHE OF YOUR LIFE

Religious reformer Martin Luther observed, "There are three conversions necessary: the conversion of the heart, the mind, and the purse." Of the three, the purse can be the most difficult for some. Especially in marriage. Agreeing on money matters is always an emotional proposition, and for many couples, tithes and offerings present a special challenge.

A fundamental shift of attitude toward giving took place in our home when we changed the question we were asking of each other. Rather than, "How much of our money should we give to God?" we learned to ask, "How much of God's money should we spend on ourselves?" The difference between these two questions was monumental for us. It helped us to remember that our financial resources are not part ours and part God's. Our income is *all* God's (see Job 41:11; Ex. 19:5–6; Ps. 24:1). With this understanding as a starting point, we eliminated much of the legalistic thinking and guilt related to giving based on a set percentage of income. John Wesley understood this when he said, "Gain all you can, save all you can, give all you can."

Another principle that has helped us comes from 2 Corinthians 8, where we are told how the Macedonians gave. Paul writes: "For I testify that they gave as much as they were able, and even beyond their ability. Entirely on their own, they urgently pleaded with

us for the privilege of sharing in this service to the Lord's people"
(8:3-4). They gave voluntarily, not because somebody twisted
their arms behind their backs. They wanted to share in the joy of
helping. A little later in that same letter, the apostle encourages
this spirit of voluntary spontaneity in giving: "Each of you should
give what you have decided in your heart to give, not reluctantly
or under compulsion, for God loves a cheerful giver" (9:7).

Why is our motivation in giving so important? Well, consider the
Pharisees and teachers of the law who used tithing to camouflage
their selfishness. They were so ritualistic about tithing that they
would count the small herbs in their garden to be sure they were
tithing on all they had. Of course, they were missing the whole point.
Listen to what Jesus said to them: "Woe to you, teachers of the law
and Pharisees, you hypocrites! You give a tenth of your spices—
mint, dill and cumin. But you have neglected the more important
matters of the law—justice, mercy and faithfulness. You should
have practiced the latter, without neglecting the former. You blind
guides! You strain out a gnat but swallow a camel" (Matt. 23:23-24).

The point of tithing, of giving a portion of your income to support
the ministry of the church, is not to keep a legalistic checklist and to
compulsively count out "God's part." The point is that we are simply
stewards of all he has given us. And by giving a portion of what he has
given us, we become converted *from* money and converted *to* him.

Here's the bottom line. The Bible calls us to "profane" the god
of money by giving it away. And to do that, we must take Christ's
famous exhortation and apply it to our checkbooks: "Where your
treasure is," Jesus said, "there your heart will be also" (Matt. 6:21).

FROM GOD'S WORD

"Will a mere mortal rob God? Yet you rob me." But you ask,
"How are we robbing you?" "In tithes and offerings. You are

under a curse—your whole nation—because you are robbing me. Bring the whole tithe into the storehouse, that there may be food in my house. Test me in this," says the Lord Almighty, "and see if I will not throw open the floodgates of heaven and pour out so much blessing that there will not be room enough to store it."

MALACHI 3:8–10

YOUR TURN

- Jesus counsels us not to "store up treasures on earth." How do you understand and live out this concept?
- Give an example of a time when you identified a financial need and gave as a team to help meet that need.
- What struggles have you encountered in trying to agree on joint giving? What are you doing to resolve them?
- Take some time to conduct a financial inventory. Identify any changes you might make in the ways you spend and give money as a couple.
- In practical and specific terms, how can the two of you more effectively share in the joy of giving?

SOUL TO SOUL

To deepen your spiritual intimacy this next week, make note of:

- What you gained from this session together.
- A pressure point in your partner's upcoming week you will pray about.
- A concrete kindness you can offer your partner this week.

PRAYER

Gracious God, we know you value generosity because you gave so much and you have promised to bless and refresh us when we give. You have even linked our kindness to those in need with the greatest honor of all: ministry to you, our Creator and King. Grant us a spirit of gladness in giving together and always make us generous. Amen.

Real-Life Soul Mates

Intimacy is about sharing all of life together. It is like unlocking all of the doors of who you are. There are no secrets. Privacy may be granted but is never protected as a right.

Since we grew up together and started dating in high school, we have known each other very well for all of our lives. But we have worked at keeping up-to-date. Intimacy has a short shelf life.

Every morning we talk to each other about plans for the day. Often we have prayed through each other's schedule. Whenever possible we call each other during the day for a minute or more of sharing. Sometimes it is only to say "I love you!" If the other doesn't answer, a message of hello and love is left on voice mail. We have often stopped by each other's places of work during the day. When Charleen was a bank teller, Leith drove by her drive-up window. Charleen often stops by Leith's office days in a row. At night we review all the day held. It has no feeling of reporting or accountability, but sharing of genuine interest in each other.

Perhaps the best times have been early in the morning before the phone rings or children are up. We each pray, often holding hands as we talk to God. We sense that all of life is open and known to God and each other, and we enjoy knowing that the partnership is three-way.

When the crises of life have come they have been surrounded with hours of talking them through. We have prayed together often. Sometimes it is not both taking a turn but one blessing the other. When his father died Leith cried, and Charleen held him and prayed for him and blessed him.

It isn't so much that there is a piece of our relationship that is spiritual or that is intimate. All of life is deliberately shared with each other and with God.

Leith and Charleen Anderson

Session Forty-One

AVOIDING THE NUMBER ONE MARRIAGE PROBLEM

"You're not listening to me!"

We hear this statement more than any other when counseling couples. No surprise. The number one marriage problem reported by couples is a breakdown of communication.

A sage once said that the Lord gave us two ears and one mouth, and that ratio ought to tell us something. Good point. We often think about "good communication skills" as learning to express ourselves more clearly, getting our message across. However, 98 percent of good communication is listening.

Listening is not passive. It is not sitting back, quietly hearing what our partner has to say, waiting for our turn to talk. Listening is active. It is getting involved with your partner's message to accurately understand it. The point of active listening is to let your partner know you are in tune with him or her. That's all. A good listener doesn't give advice or try to solve problems with sermons and testimonies. A good listener listens.

Consider this typical interaction:

Wife: I don't know what to tell Melody. She wanted to
ride with us to the game this weekend and I said okay,

but then I remembered I had already invited Tim and Sarah.

Husband: Um-m.

Wife: So what should we do?

Husband: About what?

Wife: About Melody. There's not enough room for her to ride with us.

Husband: Well, then she can't ride with us. Just call her and tell her.

Wife: I know. I know. But . . . you don't understand.

Husband: I'm listening.

Is he really? We don't think so. He may be hearing his wife's words, but he is not understanding his wife's feelings. She is not wanting him to solve her problem as much as she is wanting him to understand how lousy she feels. If he were actively listening, he would have said something like, "Sounds like you are afraid of hurting Melody's feelings." That's all. No fix-it solutions. Simply identifying the real message is what listening is about.

Jesus understood the importance of listening. Even as a young boy he sat with the teachers in the temple, "listening to them and asking them questions [and] everyone . . . was amazed at his understanding" (Luke 2:46–47). The apostle Paul understood that listening requires diligent work. When he was before Agrippa, he said, "I beg you to listen to me patiently" (Acts 26:3). The book of James tells us to "be quick to listen, slow to speak" (James 1:19). And the book of Proverbs says, "To answer before listening—that is folly and shame" (18:13).

The word *listen* occurs more than two hundred times in the Bible. It is a practice that is essential to all relationships and especially marriage. So the next time you are eager to quickly solve your partner's problems, make sure you first understand his or her feelings.

FROM GOD'S WORD

A false witness will perish, but a careful listener will testify successfully. The wicked put up a bold front, but the upright give thought to their ways.

PROVERBS 21:28–29

YOUR TURN

- Why do you think the Bible so often emphasizes the ability to listen? Why does it single it out as a mark of wisdom?
- What is one thing you would like your partner to understand about your need to be listened to and understood? How would you like him or her to improve as a listener?
- Give an example of how you benefited from a recent time of communication with your partner—a time when he or she was an especially good listener.
- When do you most often want to be listened to by your partner? How do you convey this to him or her? Or do you?
- Do you feel that gender differences help or complicate listening? Give examples to support your comments.

SOUL TO SOUL

To deepen your spiritual intimacy this next week, make note of:

- What you gained from this session together.
- A pressure point in your partner's upcoming week you will pray about.
- A concrete kindness you can offer your partner this week.

PRAYER

Gracious God, refresh our lives with the strength of your Son. Let your presence be real in our minds and hearts. Direct us as we speak and listen. Help us to stay tuned in to our partner. Deepen our listening skills and guide us in ways we may become more sensitive to each other this week. Amen.

Real-Life Soul Mates

John, a young husband in our congregation, came to us one day filled with enthusiasm. He had discovered in Hebrews 4:15 that Jesus is "touched with our feelings." That expression from the old King James Version had exploded like a holy light upon him and his wife, Ruby.

He exclaimed, "Pastor Jack and Anna, we've found a secret. Our arguments have suddenly begun to find quicker conclusions. Instead of analyzing what the other said, we've started feeling.

"I suddenly saw," he explained, "how Jesus feels the hurt of what bothers me, rather than complaining about my inadequacy or failure. This reminded me of Ephesians 5:25, and how it says I am to love my wife like Jesus loves the church."

This young man, ten years our junior, couldn't know how his insight helped us! And while our twenty years of marriage (at that time) had never held less than a full will to resolve all difficulties with loving commitment, something changed with our grasp of this concept. We found that feelings, not analyzing—the mind-wearying dissecting of words and meanings, situations and circumstances—cut more quickly to the core of problems in communication.

Now, when anything tough tests our patience with each other, we refuse to argue from logic, but rather allow ourselves to be "touched" with each other's feelings. Often, sitting with cups of tea at a winter fireside, we'll elaborate on the feelings we experienced—and the lessons they teach us about each other. The mood of such interchange is filled with discovery as we learn to be like Jesus toward each other—"touched with the feelings of our weaknesses."

Jack and Anna Hayford

Session Forty-Two

THE ATTITUDE OF GRATITUDE

"Thanks," said Les. I had just handed him a stack of mail I picked up at his office.

"You bet," I replied without giving it a second thought.

"No, I mean it—thank you," Les said with all seriousness. "It was really thoughtful of you to pick up my mail and bring it home. You didn't have to do it, and I appreciate it."

It's always nice to be around somebody who's grateful. Cicero, the Roman philosopher, said, "Gratitude is not only the greatest of virtues, but the parent of all the others." When we are grateful—when we have an attitude of gratitude—we become better people.

Saying "thank you" tends to diminish over the years of marriage as we take each other more for granted. One group of social scientists discovered that the phrases *shhh* and *what's on* are more common in most homes than *thank you*.

Scripture abounds with encouragement to be thankful. "Let the peace of Christ rule in your hearts, since as members of one body you were called to peace. And be *thankful*" (Col. 3:15, italics added). "*Giving joyful thanks* to the Father, who has qualified you to share in the inheritance of his holy people in the kingdom of light" (Col. 1:12, italics added). "Do not be anxious about anything, but in every situation, by prayer and petition, *with thanksgiving*, present your requests to God" (Phil. 4:6, italics added). The apostle Paul advised the church at Thessalonica: "*Give thanks* in all circumstances, for this is God's will for you in Christ Jesus" (1 Thess. 5:18, italics added). Scripture also tells us that thankfulness is a prerequisite for worship: "Enter his gates *with thanksgiving* and his courts with praise; *give thanks*" (Ps. 100:4, italics added).

To understand what it means to have the attitude of gratitude, we can start with a verse from the book of Hebrews. You may think at first that it has nothing to do with gratitude, but take a moment to read it.

Therefore, since we are receiving a kingdom which cannot be shaken, let us have grace, by which we may serve God acceptably with reverence and godly fear. (Heb. 12:28 NKJV)

There is a remarkable difference between this translation of the passage and the translation found in the New International Version. Where the New King James Version says, "Let us have grace," the NIV says, "Let us be thankful." Each of these translations, however, is correct because in Greek, *charis*, "to have grace," also means "thank you."

Grace and thankfulness are connected. In giving thanks we receive grace. In other words, we cannot enjoy God's grace without being thankful. And we cannot be in good graces with our partner if we are not grateful.

So keep the attitude of gratitude alive in your marriage. Cultivate it by looking for things to appreciate in your partner each day. After all, gratitude really is the parent of all virtues.

FROM GOD'S WORD

Always strive to do what is good for each other and for everyone else. Rejoice always, pray continually, give thanks in all circumstances; for this is God's will for you in Christ Jesus.

1 Thessalonians 5:15–18

YOUR TURN

- Many times the Scriptures talk about being thankful. Why do you think the virtue of gratitude is highlighted so often in the Bible?
- What is it about your partner that makes you the most thankful?
- Give an example of a recent time when your partner, out of courtesy, said "thank you" and it gave you a little boost.
- So often our gratitude goes unspoken. We feel grateful, but we just don't say it. Share with your partner some "thank you"s you have been withholding.
- Take an inventory of the strengths of your marriage. How often do you give thanks to God for these gifts?

SOUL TO SOUL

To deepen your spiritual intimacy this next week, make note of:

- What you gained from this session together.
- A pressure point in your partner's upcoming week you will pray about.
- A concrete kindness you can offer your partner this week.

PRAYER

Generous Father, teach us day by day the deep rewards of gratitude. Help us to experience fully the gifts we have in one another—and enable us to make known our thankfulness to each other in such a way that it energizes and enriches our marriage this week. We thank you for all your blessings. Amen.

Real-Life Soul Mates

A peaceful, meandering river runs through our town, with a paved path on either side of it that runs miles in either direction. Sue and I have savored that river for almost three decades—biking it, kayaking it, but mostly enjoying leisurely walks alongside of it. Walking gives us the best opportunity to talk and catch up with each other.

Like most married couples with kids, much of our conversation revolves around how our children are doing. At some point in the past, the realization dawned on us that we should do less talking and more praying about these concerns. So our regular strolls along the river became prayer walks.

Not that we pray the entire time. We still do a lot of catching up with each other before we kick into intercession. But we've made it a rule: *Talk on the mile-and-a-half route upriver. Then cross at the Fabyan Park Bridge and pray on the return trip to town.* While this rule has served us well in developing a shared prayer life, over time we noticed an unpleasant tendency developing. Our prayers for our kids often slipped into a sort of hand-wringing.

You know what I'm talking about if you're a parent. You start appealing to God on behalf of your children—whether about their dating relationships, or their request for a tattoo, or their anxiety attacks, or their spiritual life—and it's so easy for that appeal to become a whiny entreaty. Sue and I were becoming whiners. Rather than being refreshed at the end of our prayer walks, having left our children in God's hands, we frequently concluded our intercession with a heightened sense of unease about their well-being.

It was time for us to start employing one of the practices that I teach in my book *Prayer Coach.* I call it "thank-you therapy." This discipline comes out of Philippians 4:6–7, which says: "Do not be anxious about anything, but in every situation, by prayer and petition, with thanksgiving, present your requests to God. And the peace of God . . . will guard your hearts and your minds." The key phrase in those two verses is: "with thanksgiving." When we pray *without* thanksgiving, our anxiety often increases. But when we accompany each petition with a heartfelt expression of gratitude for something we see God doing in that situation, God's peace settles over us.

So we're still walking the river—often several times a week, in good weather or bad (and in Chicagoland, *bad* can mean snow and ice). And we still catch up with each other going upstream, and pray going downstream. But now we insist that our intercession be wrapped in thanksgiving. What an inspiring combo: a scenic river, a faithful partner, and an intimate connection with God.

Jim and Sue Nicodem

Session Forty-Three

WHO'S IN CHARGE HERE?

Tim, a young man, recently married, invited me (Les) to lunch one day and asked, "How can I get my wife to submit to me?" His question threw me. I have counseled many newlyweds, but I had never heard the question phrased so bluntly.

Tim was a devout Christian trying to build his new marriage on biblical principles, and he wanted to be the "head" of the home. He read about headship in the verse that says, "The husband is the head of the wife as Christ is the head of the church, his body, of which he is the Savior" (Eph. 5:23). Tim interpreted this statement to mean literally that it was his job to be the boss of his wife. And it was her job to be submissive to his demands. Tim's wife, however, didn't see things that way because she lived in the twentieth century, not the first. She saw herself, understandably, as an equal partner in the marriage.

Tim, sincere as he was, didn't fully understand what it meant to be "the head of his wife as Christ is the head of the church." It never seemed to occur to Tim that in the Bible the husband is never called to make his wife submit. The Bible doesn't call husbands to rule over their lives but to renounce the desire to be master. Out of reverence for Christ, husbands should be the first to honor and respect their wives.

What then is headship? Let me tell you what I told Tim. Headship is not being the first in line. It is not being the boss or ruler. It is being the first to honor, the first to nurture, the first to meet your partner's needs.

A healthy marriage is built on a mutual desire to submit one's needs to the other. As Ephesians 5:21 says: "Submit to one another out of reverence for Christ." That's the basic principle. Emptying ourselves of our self-centered desires is the bridge to becoming soul mates. Without mutual submission every marriage, no matter how romantic, will eventually falter. As Amos 3:3 says, "Do two walk together unless they have agreed to do so?"

Remember the Aesop's fable in which the wind and the sun argued over which was the stronger? The wind said, "Do you see that old man down there? I can make him take his coat off quicker than you can."

The sun agreed to go behind a cloud while the wind blew up a storm. However, the harder the wind blew, the firmer the old man wrapped his coat around him. Eventually the wind gave up and the sun came out from behind the cloud and smiled kindly upon the old man. Before long, the man mopped his brow, pulled off his coat, and strolled along his way. The sun knew the secret: Warmth and a gentle touch are always stronger than force and fury.

If we worry about our partner submitting to us, we have not grasped this important principle. Like a blowing wind, our good intentions wreak havoc on our partner and our marriage. The key is understanding that submission is a two-way street in marriage. Scripture not only calls husbands and wives to "submit to one another" (Eph. 5:21), but we are to also submit to God (see Job 22:21; Heb. 12:9; James 4:7).

FROM GOD'S WORD

Wives, submit to your husbands as you do to the Lord. For the husband is the head of the wife as Christ is the head of the church, his body, of which he is the Savior. Now as the church submits to Christ, so also wives should submit to their husbands in everything. Husbands, love your wives, just as Christ loved the church and gave himself up for her to make her holy. . . . In this same way, husbands ought to love their wives as their own bodies. He who loves his wife loves himself.

Ephesians 5:22–26, 28

YOUR TURN

- How does your faith enable you to practice mutual submission in your marriage and how does your marriage teach you about submitting to God?
- How was the principle of mutual submission modeled in your family growing up?
- It is difficult to submit to another's needs if you are unaware of them. Talk about how the two of you make your needs known to each other (i.e., are you direct, indirect, emotional, rational, etc.?).
- Give an example of a time when each of you practiced mutual submission.
- In most marriages the wife makes some decisions, the husband makes others. But then there are some matters that are so important that they require both husband and wife. What are some examples of these important issues for you?

SOUL TO SOUL

To deepen your spiritual intimacy this next week, make note of:

- What you gained from this session together.
- A pressure point in your partner's upcoming week you will pray about.
- A concrete kindness you can offer your partner this week.

PRAYER

Merciful God, empty us of our self-centered desires and grant us the willingness to submit our needs to each other. Help us to discern the two-way street of mutual submission in our marriage as we build up our love and become soul mates. And God, teach us daily to submit to you. Amen.

Real-Life Soul Mates

I'm a dreamer. Dreaming about what God is up to and what he has planned for us is one of my favorite things to do. I'm not a very structured person. I am a creative type, which for me usually means living in the free-flowing moment. Even writing a piece like this is stressful to me.

When my wife Kandice and I were first married, I put a lot of pressure on myself as the husband. I felt since it was my responsibility to be head of the household—leader of the family—that it was on me to get us from point A to point B in life. The way that had always worked in my life was trusting God and flying by the seat of my pants.

Out of a well-meaning but ignorant idea of how I was supposed to lead, I tried to share the dreams of what I felt God was putting on my heart for our family. I'd then relate a very incomplete plan of how I thought we were going to get there. You know how they say opposites attract? Well, it couldn't be any truer for me and my Kandice.

Unlike me, Kandice is a very structured person and a really great planner. She would instantly have lots of obvious questions about my very vague plan. (Which wasn't really a plan at all since I was only dreaming for the future in the first place.) I interpreted these questions as a lack of faith in my ability or in God and would either become very defensive or shut down altogether. Kandice has a to-do list. She is a very structured, get-it-done person. She is one of the most incredibly productive people I have ever met, and I marvel at her ability to accomplish huge tasks. As I shared dreams for the future, most of what she heard were items to add to her already very full to-do list. When it felt to me that she was "pushing back" with her questions, my insecurity screamed inside, "It's because you're not being a strong enough leader" or "You're not man enough for this job."

In reality, Kandice wasn't going to catch the dream because I talked her into it. God would have to show her in due time if the vision was what he wanted for our family. As a couple, we learned that God is never the cause for argument or strife! Kandice is learning to patiently (and sometimes not so patiently) listen to what God shows me, and then she shares with me in the same way.

I'm learning how to rest in the vision the Lord has shown me for our family, but to hold that loosely and realize that if it really is him, that he'll show Kandice too. And if it's not, then we really don't want it anyway. Either way we are enjoying the process together, now eager to see how God leads us forward.

Mike and Kandice Weaver

Session Forty-Four

GOD'S PERFECT LOVE

In the opening scene of *Oliver*, the musical based on the Charles Dickens novel *Oliver Twist*, destitute boys in a London orphanage hover over a miserable meal of gruel. Meanwhile, the family and friends of the manager enjoy heaping platters of succulent fowl and tasty vegetables in an adjoining dining room that the boys can see. Although the paint is peeling on the stark gray wall behind the rough tables where the boys are sitting, a huge motto dares to show itself: GOD IS LOVE.

The audience is left to wonder whether the ragged, coughing urchins ever notice the dusty sign, let alone comprehend its meaning. But in reality, God's love is not part of a theatrical backdrop. It is not meant to have a paradoxical place onstage. God's love is real. It is living and breathing in you and your partner.

How you perceive God's love shapes your love for each other. God's love is self-sacrificing (John 15:13), unchangeable (John 13:1), and compelling (2 Cor. 5:14). God's love is also jealous (Ex. 20:5; 34:14; Deut. 4:25; 5:9; 6:15). This may sound strange to modern ears, but there is a beautiful idea behind this kind of "jealous" love. To say that God is a jealous God is to say that God is the lover of men and women, and that his heart can have no rival. He must have the whole devotion of our hearts. The divine-human relationship is not that of king and subject, nor that of master and servant, nor that of owner and slave, nor that of judge and defendant, but that of lover and loved one, a relationship which can only be paralleled in the perfect marriage relationship between husband and wife.

"When I stop to think of all that love should be—accepting, forgiving, supporting, strengthening—God is all that and more," wrote Ruth Bell Graham. "He is perfect love." And when Ruth Graham felt that her love for her husband Billy did not measure up to such divine standards, she said: "At that moment Romans 8:31–39 comes into my consciousness, and I am surrounded again by an awareness of God's love. He loves me in spite of me!" Have you ever felt like your love is not all you want it to be? You're not alone. Only God's love is perfect. So as you begin the journey of becoming soul mates, pray that you will be "filled to the measure of all the fullness of God" (Eph. 3:19).

If the GOD IS LOVE sign had the audacity to cling to the scaly wall in Oliver's dreadful orphanage, it can surely abide in the hearts of a husband and wife who care for each other.

FROM GOD'S WORD

Who shall separate us from the love of Christ? Shall trouble or hardship or persecution or famine or nakedness or danger or sword? . . . No, in all these things we are more than conquerors through him who loved us. For I am convinced that neither death nor life, neither angels nor demons, neither the present nor the future, nor any powers, neither height nor depth, nor anything else in all creation, will be able to separate us from the love of God that is in Christ Jesus our Lord.

ROMANS 8:35–39

YOUR TURN

- How does God's love, as expressed in the Romans passage, shape your love for your partner?
- Give an example of how you have recently encountered God's love demonstrated in your marriage through your partner's actions.
- Discuss how God's love can sustain you in marriage even when one of you falls short of the mark on love.
- What is one way you and your partner can seek to become more "rooted and established in God's love"?
- Why do you think God's love is described as an "unchangeable" love? How does this inform your approach to loving your partner?

SOUL TO SOUL

To deepen your spiritual intimacy this next week, make note of:

- What you gained from this session together.
- A pressure point in your partner's upcoming week you will pray about.
- A concrete kindness you can offer your partner this week.

PRAYER

Gracious God, lover of our souls, we ask you to reveal your love to us as a couple. Show us your love for us as individuals through our partner's loving actions. And teach us to love as you do. We aspire to live a life that reflects your love, allowing you to transform our marriage into one of rare character. Thank you for a love from which nothing can separate us. Amen.

Real-Life Soul Mates

When we got married we asked a question that you're probably asking, too: "How do we have a great marriage?" We didn't want to settle for second best. After all, we fell madly in love with each other, and when we married in 1994, we married for life—and we wanted to honor God in this relationship. So right from the start we knew that walking together with God would be central to our marriage.

That's why we've worked to view our lives and build our marriage through an "eternal lens."

Because I am crazy about Lisa, I want her to have a great life. But more than that, I want her to have a great eternity. I want her to look back at her life without regret. I want her to be confident that the time she spent on earth prepared her for heaven. Most importantly, I want her to hear God say, "Well done, good and faithful servant! You have been faithful with a few things; I will put you in charge of many things. Come and share your master's happiness!" (Matt. 25:23).

A strange thing happened when Lisa and I started living with an eternal lens: it caused us to enjoy the here and now! Many people will tell you to focus on your marriage, to focus on each other; but we discovered that focusing on God's mission made our marriage amazing. This caused us to experience Jesus deeply—what could be better?

Eternal-mindedness keeps us from silly arguments. There's no time to fight. We have better things to pursue than our own selfish interests. Too much is at stake! God created us for a purpose. We can't afford to waste our lives. We can't afford to waste our marriage by merely pursuing our own happiness.

But let me warn you. A Christ-centered and eternity-minded marriage is not the same thing as a "fun" marriage. Lisa and I have a blast together, but some of the decisions we make are painful. Yet we know they are right. Christ promises the abundant life (John 10:10), but that is not always synonymous with fun. But tough decisions made for God's glory produce a good and right pain, a pain that believers are meant to endure in this fallen world. It's a pain that makes us stronger, holier, more in love with God and each other. Any suffering for his sake is a constant reminder of our future where all the pain will be exchanged for glory.

Francis and Lisa Chan

THE GUILT-FREE DROP

Early in my career, I (Les) attended a conference on laughter in the ballroom of the Disneyland Hotel. Dr. Steve Allen Jr., the son of the famous comedian, handed out three scarves and then went through about a dozen steps to teach this room full of psychologists the art of juggling. The first step was to hold one of the scarves out at arm's length—and drop it.

Everyone thought he was joking. Nobody dropped their scarf. "C'mon now, drop it!" Dr. Allen commanded. One by one, people reluctantly released their scarves and they fluttered to the carpeted floor. "There now, doesn't that feel better?" asked Dr. Allen. "You have gotten your mistake over with. This is the first step in learning to juggle. We call it the guilt-free drop."

Isn't that a wonderful principle? Do you need a guilt-free drop? Does your partner? Well, Les doesn't juggle that often, but we apply the guilt-free drop to our marriage almost daily.

Marriage offers a lot of opportunities for partners to feel guilty. In a survey assessing "who makes you feel most guilty," the majority of respondents confessed they were the key perpetrators of their own guilt. But next on the list was "my spouse."

Research has also revealed that much of the guilt we experience is undeserved. We endure false guilt when we suffer self-punishment needlessly. Our internal tape recorder says, "You should *always* have the house clean," "You should *never* come home late," or "You should *never* make a mistake."

Each of us is born with a judge and jury on the inside. We are in the courtroom daily, waiting to hear the verdict: Guilty or not guilty? Not that the decision has any bearing on the truth. It is our emotions, and not reality, that often determine the verdict. For at the root of self-imposed guilt is the idea that what you feel must be true—or, in other words, if you *feel* guilty, you think you must have *done* something wrong. However, emotions can lie, because they are not products of reality, but of our *interpretation* of reality. The psalmist alludes to this when he says, "Troubles without number surround me; my sins have overtaken me, and I cannot see" (40:12).

Feelings of guilt cause blurry vision. That's why it is important for soul mates to give one another a guilt-free drop now and then. We need to offer grace to each other. We need to help each other see reality as it is, so that we can avoid needless self-punishment.

Of course, the saddest form of false guilt comes in not believing in and accepting God's grace and forgiveness. Paul writes to the Romans: "Therefore, there is now no condemnation for those who are in Christ Jesus, because through Christ Jesus the law of the Spirit who gives life has set you free from the law of sin and death" (8:1). God sent his Son to earth not just to give us a guilt-free drop, but to give us a guilt-free life.

FROM GOD'S WORD

Even if I caused you sorrow by my letter, I do not regret it. Though I did regret it—I see that my letter hurt you, but only for a little while—yet now I am happy, not because you were made sorry, but because your sorrow led you to repentance. For you became sorrowful as God intended and so were not harmed in any way by us. Godly sorrow brings repentance that leads to salvation and leaves no regret, but worldly sorrow [guilt] brings death.

2 CORINTHIANS 7:8–10

YOUR TURN

- Some Christians believe that God wants them to feel guilty. Do you have a hard time believing that there is "no condemnation for those who are in Christ Jesus"?
- Give an example of a time in your life when you were afforded grace instead of guilt. What did that do for you?
- Discuss the difference between true guilt and false guilt and how both affect marriage.
- When are you most tempted to make your mate feel guilty? Why?
- Talk about some real-life situations where you might give one another a "guilt-free drop."

SOUL TO SOUL

To deepen your spiritual intimacy this next week, make note of:

- What you gained from this session together.
- A pressure point in your partner's upcoming week you will pray about.
- A concrete kindness you can offer your partner this week.

PRAYER

Our Father, help us to live in the fullness and light of your salvation rather than under the dark shadow of guilt. Lift the quality of our life together. Show us your grace daily in our lives and teach us to give ourselves to each other. Grant us a marriage without condemnation. Amen.

Real-Life Soul Mates

Keith Moore and I were a train wreck. I cannot fathom how two high-functioning people could have been more inwardly fouled up. We'd earned it. He'd come from a family traumatized early on by a tragedy so terrible that they were scarred for life. I'd come from early childhood victimization, an atmosphere of addiction, and unrelenting instability. Our attraction was so strong that Keith and I each broke off long-term relationships that were headed to the marriage altar in order to marry each other. Our version of a unity candle may as well have been a match set to two strands of firecrackers. One of the mysteries of the heart is how on earth it is capable of both loving and hating the same exact person with equal intensity.

Even though I'd accepted Christ in childhood and surrendered to vocational ministry at eighteen, I still somehow thought the only qualification necessary for two people to be equally yoked was for both to be Christians. I told Keith I could only marry him if he became a Christian, so he did. I smile as I write these words: I'm not sure if Keith asked Jesus into his heart at that time or me. Nevertheless, it was the only qualification on my checklist, and once it was scratched off the list, down the aisle we went.

To the grace and glory of Jesus Christ alone, we will soon celebrate thirty-nine years together. And I do mean *celebrate*. That's what you do to commemorate miracles. We'll be able to say with all honesty and probably with tears stinging our eyes, "I'd choose you again." That day we'd said, "I do," I'd been absolutely certain he'd become a leader in the church, surely a deacon, but he became neither. What he became for me was a guarantee of authenticity. What he became for me was a man I could not manipulate, control, or spiritually regulate. What he became for me was a house of mirrors. I was forced to face the fact at every turn that I had tremendous brokenness in my life that only Jesus could mend. What Keith became for me was my introduction to grace and ultimately my deliverance from legalism.

Our spiritual intimacy looks different than more exemplary Christian couples. What we have to offer is not necessarily a how-to. It would lean a bit more heavily toward a how-not-to. What Keith and I hope is that we can be hope to those who, despite doing it all wrong, wanted to stay together and make it work. We can't offer a how-to-marry approach but maybe we could take a shot at offering a how-to-stay-married approach. We have cried out to Jesus both together and separately. We have worked hard. We have fought hard. We have forgiven hard. We've humbled ourselves before one another over and over again and owned our own problems and asked for help and sought godly counsel. This one is huge: we've had to accept one another *as we are*. Strangely, God getting through to us to quit trying to change the other one and instead accept him/her just like we were, *this* was the very process that created an environment for us to slowly change. Then, over time and commitment, something shifted.

We're still as different as night and day, Keith and I. We still see many things differently, but we see them glued side-by-side. For a man who never did become a church leader or a deacon, nobody on the planet has shown me the grace of Jesus Christ like Keith Moore. Nobody has supported me more or believed more forthrightly in what God called me to do. Nobody makes me laugh more. Somehow God gave Keith and me the gift of finding one another hilarious. I'm not sure how much Keith prays on his own—I gave up regulating those things long ago—but he prays over me every time I speak or teach. He prays over our children and speaks words of blessing over them. Keith and I take long walks through the woods by our house, hold hands and talk about how God rescued us and how he's graced us. These are the things of spiritual intimacy to Keith and me. We don't do devotions together like many other couples or read the Bible together or pray together on a regular basis except over meals. I wanted those things so badly for so long but I had to quit comparing us to other couples and, instead, find contentment in who he and I are. And this is who we are: Mr. and Mrs. Keith Moore. Thirty-nine years and counting.

Keith and Beth Moore

Session Forty-Six

STOP STEWING AND START DOING

A University of Michigan study determined that 60 percent of human worries are totally unwarranted. Of the remaining portion of our worries, 20 percent are about things already past and activities completely beyond our control. Another 10 percent are so petty that they don't make much difference at all. Of the remaining 10 percent of our worries, only 4 to 5 percent are really justifiable. And even half of this residue of viable worries is beyond our capacity to change! The final half, or 2 percent of our worries which are real, can be solved easily, according to these researchers, "if we stop stewing and start doing!"

The precision of these statistics is not important. The indisputable point is that most of our worries are not worth the stress they generate. How many times have the two of you let worry cloud your dinner conversation? How often do you lie awake at night consumed with an obsessive worry?

You don't have to let the poison of worry contaminate your marriage. God wants to cleanse you from needless concerns. Long ago the apostle Paul wrote that we are to stop perpetually worrying about even one thing. And he gave us a prescription for inoculating ourselves against worry in Philippians 4:4–7:

Rejoice in the Lord always. I will say it again: Rejoice! Let your
gentleness be evident to all. The Lord is near. Do not be anxious
about anything, but in every situation, by prayer and petition, with
thanksgiving, present your requests to God. And the peace of
God, which transcends all understanding, will guard your hearts
and your minds in Christ Jesus.

You want to be free from worry? Bring your concerns to
God with an attitude of thanksgiving. Don't try to figure out
everything. How this prescription for worry sickness works,
Paul says, is beyond understanding. But be assured of this, it
does work.

Jesus Christ came to give us eternal life, but also abundant
life (see John 10:10). He came to give us life to the fullest and
to set us free from the harmful effects of worry. By the way,
Jesus practiced what he preached. When faced with the hostility
of Herod and the pressure of the public clamor for healing, for
example, he had plenty to worry about. Instead, Scripture tells
us, he and the disciples took rest. Jesus said to his disciples:
"Come with me by yourselves to a quiet place and get some rest"
(Mark 6:31).

So don't allow worry to get a foothold in your marriage. Life
is too short. The possibilities are too great. Instead, as soul mates,
you can help each other to "cast all your anxiety on him because
he cares for you" (1 Peter 5:7).

FROM GOD'S WORD

Then Jesus said to his disciples: "Therefore I tell you, do not worry
about your life, what you will eat; or about your body, what you
will wear. For life is more than food, and the body more than

clothes. Consider the ravens: They do not sow or reap, they have no storeroom or barn; yet God feeds them. And how much more valuable you are than birds! Who of you by worrying can add a single hour to your life? Since you cannot do this very little thing, why do you worry about the rest?"

LUKE 12:22–26

YOUR TURN

- Why does Scripture tell us to not be anxious about anything?
- In what ways has your marriage suffered as a result of worry?
- What recurring issues tend to cause the most anxiety and worry for each of you?
- Give an example of a time when you experienced peace rather than anxiety in the face of fearful circumstances. What made it so?
- How can you help each other release worry and rely on Christ for peace and provision?

SOUL TO SOUL

To deepen your spiritual intimacy this next week, make note of:

- What you gained from this session together.
- A pressure point in your partner's upcoming week you will pray about.
- A concrete kindness you can offer your partner this week.

PRAYER

God, we acknowledge the frailty of our humanness by the unnecessary load of worry we carry. Teach us a way to live without self-defeating worry. Thank you for bearing our burdens. Help us to live in more peace and tranquillity than we did last week and the week before. Help us find the more excellent way. Amen.

Real-Life Soul Mates

Our sons are grown now, but as parents of active young children, we found that often daily crises interfered with our attempts to have a scheduled spiritual life with each other. So we learned to use the needs, problems, and joys of each day to bring ourselves and our children closer to God.

Once, at two in the morning, John drove three-year-old Ricky to the emergency room as a code three croup, gasping for breath with blocked airways. God was our only hope, and we found ourselves drawn much closer to him and each other. We often point to that event as a time we learned much about actively depending on him.

Often we saw God through our children. Once, two-year-old Benny slipped away from Barbi at a large school gathering. Panicked, she searched until she finally found him toddling in a hallway, lost in a sea of grown-up legs and torsos. When Benny spotted Barbi, he wailed and held up his arms for her to rescue him. Later, when Barbi told John the story, we were moved by how much like Benny we ourselves are: needing God's presence and comfort.

We were always concerned with what we were transferring to our next generation: Would it be our sins and dysfunctional patterns or our mature character traits? One night, as our two sons fought in the kitchen, we worried about their "bad attitudes," that is, until we realized that their squabbling style was identical to ours! As we realized our twofold task of stopping generational sin patterns and developing mature character in our kids, we felt much more of a need to confess, repent, and ask forgiveness for our own immaturities.

We struggled as imperfect, unfinished parents, asking God and each other to help us grow each other up so we could help our boys grow up. As we look back now, we are so thankful that he faithfully answered those prayers.

John and Barbi Townsend

SINKING YOUR ROOTS DOWN DEEP

If you are like most couples in America, you won't live in one place very long. In an average year, some forty million Americans move. Put another way, every ten years, between 40 and 60 percent of an average American town's population moves in or out. And get this. The average worker only keeps a job 3.6 years. So will you lengthen your roots and stay where you are for a good long while? Probably not. If you are like most Americans, you will move about fourteen times in your lifetime.

Of course, multiple moves have not always characterized life in America. Chances are that your grandparents or great-grandparents stayed most of their adult lives in the same region, even the same house. Before our country was crisscrossed with interstate highways and before airplanes made cross-country travel easy, people stayed put a lot more than we do now. People had deep roots.

You have to work pretty hard in our high-tech society to lay down lifelong roots. It's not impossible, but it's rare. However, there is a kind of rootedness in marriage that comes from being soul mates. Allow us to illustrate it this way: The root system of most trees is as wide and deep as the leaf line is wide and high. That is not true, however, of the redwood, which has a shallow root system that spreads out in all directions. That fact of life creates a problem for a redwood standing alone. It can easily be blown over because the lack of deep roots gives it little stability. However, when two redwoods grow together, their root structures intertwine with each other and give one another strength. Though weak as separate trees, they become strong together. The same is true for soul mates. "Two are better than one," said King Solomon (Eccl. 4:9).

Whether you live in one place for many years or relocate around the country according to job requirements, the most important roots you'll ever establish are in God and his Word. For this spiritual root system will bear much fruit. "I am the vine," said Jesus, "you are the branches. If you remain in me and I in you, you will bear much fruit; apart from me you can do nothing. . . . If you remain in me and my words remain in you, ask whatever you wish, and it will be done for you. This is to my Father's glory, that you bear much fruit, showing yourselves to be my disciples" (John 15:5–8).

As a couple grows together in their understanding of God and his Word, they become all the more "rooted and established in love" (Eph. 3:17). So if your circumstances take you from coast to coast or anywhere around the world, never forget that soul mates, like the redwoods, become stronger together.

FROM GOD'S WORD

Two are better than one, because they have a good return for their labor. If either of them falls down, one can help the other up. But pity anyone who falls and has no one to help them up! Also, if two lie down together, they will keep warm. But how can one keep warm alone? Though one may be overpowered, two can defend themselves. A cord of three strands is not quickly broken.

ECCLESIASTES 4:9–12

YOUR TURN

- Christ invites us to "abide in him." What does this mean to you, and how does it nurture your spiritual root system?
- Most married couples experience times of uprooting from family or friends. What has your experience been?
- Give an example of a project or activity or experience which has "intertwined your roots" as soul mates.
- What are the goals you share as a couple that increase your rootedness in each other?
- How are the two of you growing together in an understanding of God's Word? Can you think of some specific examples?

SOUL TO SOUL

To deepen your spiritual intimacy this next week, make note of:

- What you gained from this session together.
- A pressure point in your partner's upcoming week you will pray about.
- A concrete kindness you can offer your partner this week.

PRAYER

Gracious God, the blessings that come from being rooted together in your Word are many. You have promised to make us fruitful and prosperous and to protect us from withering in the face of adversity. Teach us to delight in your Word and to draw strength from one another. Enable us to drop our roots into the rich soil of a good marriage relationship and to be established in strength together. Amen.

Real-Life Soul Mates

We believe in marriage mentoring. We believe every marriage is a duet in need of great backup singers.

For our marriage to thrive, we need voices of influence speaking truth into our hearts. Years ago, one of our backup singers said, "Your marriage needs a daily delay, a weekly withdrawal, and an annual abandon." At the time, we had no idea how that simple three-point suggestion would change everything about our marriage and walk with the Lord.

We grow closer to each other and Jesus when we spend fifteen to twenty minutes together each day in a distraction-free setting. That means no phones, technology, or children. We connect to discuss dreams, goals, issues, expectations, and what the Lord is teaching us. The goal is to get everything out on the table. Morning, noon, or night, our daily delay may take place at the table, in the family room, the breakfast nook, or the bedroom. Wherever and whenever, we take a few minutes to keep the lines of communication open.

We also prioritize a weekly date night. Our dates are fun and filled with laughter. No unresolved issues, unmet expectations, or escalated conflicts allowed. Period. When we spend quality time with each other every day, there's no need to discuss heavy topics on date night. Date night is all about enjoying life together (Eccl. 9:7–9).

Finally, the annual abandon is our couple's retreat to refresh and recalibrate. Here we ask the Lord for direction for the upcoming year. Some couples choose the mountains or the beach. We live in the Ozark Mountains near beautiful Table Rock Lake, so getting out of town for us means visiting a big city. We love walking and eating. There's nothing more refreshing for us than walking ten to twelve miles a day in the hustle and bustle of a big city and ending the day with a fine dining experience.

Quality couple time honors and prioritizes our marriage before the Lord. It is also a signal to our family and friends that says, "Our marriage is important."

Ted and Amy Cunningham

DO YOU DREAM
WHAT I DREAM?

The musical *Man of La Mancha* is one of our all-time favorites. It is the story of a crazy old man suffering from what we would now call senile psychosis.

The action takes place a hundred years after the age of chivalry when there were no more knights. But, thinking he is one, Don Quixote puts on a strange suit of armor and rides into the world to battle evil and protect the weak and powerless. He brings along his funny little servant Sancho Panza as his squire. When they arrive at a broken-down old inn used by mule traders, Don Quixote calls the innkeeper the lord of a great castle. In the inn he meets the most miserable human being imaginable, a pathetic orphan girl who does menial chores and is degraded by the mule traders. Don Quixote pronounces this wretched girl the great lady Dulcinea and begs for her handkerchief as a token to carry with him into battle.

Everyone thinks Don Quixote is bonkers, but at the end of the play the old, dying man no longer suffers from these delusions. In a moving scene, all the people he has renamed appear at his bedside and beg him not to change. His excitement about their future has transformed them, and they have become the people that this insane visionary imagined.

The message of the play is simple: The dreams and hopes of the people around us powerfully shape our lives. And the message to married couples is that what you dream for each other (and whether you dream) will powerfully shape your marriage.

We have a plaque in our home with the following inscription from Henry David Thoreau: "If one advances confidently in the direction of his dreams, and endeavors to live the life which he has imagined, he will meet with a success unexpected in common hours." What we consciously dream about, what we envision for our future together, and the goals we set for our partnership, determine the quality of our marriage in the present. For where there is no vision, a marriage will perish (see Prov. 29:18). And if our dreams are worthy and filled with godly hope, they take us to heights we never imagined.

Of course, it is possible to have dreams that are not godly. So how should a Christian couple dream according to the Bible? Consider a paraphrasing of Paul's words in Philippians 4:8: "Whatever is true, whatever is noble, whatever is right, whatever is pure, whatever is lovely, whatever is admirable—dream on those things." The focus of a healthy dream and vision is not on "laying up treasures on earth" but on pleasing God.

So learn to dream. And dream big! It was J. Oswald Sanders who rightly said, "The frontiers of the kingdom of God were never advanced by men and women of caution."

FROM GOD'S WORD

And afterward, I will pour out my Spirit on all people. Your sons and daughters will prophesy, your old men will dream dreams, your young men will see visions.

JOEL 2:28

YOUR TURN

- Scripture underscores the value of dreams and visions. Why do you think this is?
- Give an example of a time when your partner was a catalyst for something beyond your expectations—a time when he or she helped you dream.
- What are the dreams you share for your future together? How do you see your marriage, ten, twenty, thirty years from now?
- Sometimes a spouse will unknowingly shoot down a partner's dream. Has this happened to either of you? How can you prevent this from happening?
- Have you ever written down goals as a couple? If you were to note three goals for your marriage, what would they be?

SOUL TO SOUL

To deepen your spiritual intimacy this next week, make note of:

- What you gained from this session together.
- A pressure point in your partner's upcoming week you will pray about.
- A concrete kindness you can offer your partner this week.

PRAYER

God of all knowledge, fill our lives with a vision beyond this moment or this week. Help us to dream expansively for the future of our life together. May we challenge and support one another in such a way that our dreams elevate our partner to a better life. Thank you for your promise to withhold no good thing from us. We are grateful for your goodness and mercy. Amen.

Real-Life Soul Mates

Mike is all about motorcycles, Led Zeppelin, and grilled beef. Carmen is more about bicycles, James Taylor, and green salad. With such divergent personalities, activities, and interests, what could possibly get us together and keep us connected? Only Jesus.

We met in the seventies when we were seventeen years old, both new to a relationship with Jesus and attending a hippie-friendly church in Eugene, Oregon. One Sunday, when the pastor encouraged us to turn and introduce ourselves to the person next to us, a relationship was born that has lasted more than four decades—withstanding several stormy seasons that forced us to finally grow up.

Thankfully, spiritual intimacy was built into our relationship from the beginning. It is what held us together during the roughest years. In the early months of our friendship, we attended a college group where we practiced conversational prayer as an integral part of our spiritual journey. Now it's hard to imagine a day without it. We pray alone, together, and with friends and family members throughout the day. After many years of practice, prayer is now as simple, natural, and essential as breathing.

We also started serving together while we were dating. We began by entertaining two-year-olds, moved on to junior high ministry, high school ministry, college ministry, and then moved to Seattle, Washington, to plant a new church, where we stayed for seventeen years. Under less-than-perfect circumstances, we then moved to San Diego to take over a young church plant. Despite a rough transition, we have enjoyed serving here for eighteen years.

While we have never practiced the structured devotional life that some people enjoy, somewhere along the way we began a pattern of starting each day with coffee and conversation. First one up makes the coffee. Our daily discussions include everything from who will make dinner to wrestling with deep spiritual truths. Where we used to operate as individuals, we have learned to function as a team. We actively look for ways to serve and support each other at home and at work. Serving as opposed to selfishness helps our relationship thrive.

Which brings us to the present. As strange as it may sound, the way we maintain our spiritual connection in this season of life is often through silence. We enjoy taking walks, bike rides, hikes, and car trips together. (Sadly, there is no motorcycle in the garage right now.) Though we still have a lot to discuss—and can often be heard actively hashing out our issues and ideas from our different points of view—we also enjoy the deep sense of trust, familiarity, and contentment we have built with each other over the decades. Spending recreational time together—even in a comfortable silence—is a healing, restorative spiritual experience.

Mike and Carmen Meeks

A LITTLE HEAVEN
ON EARTH

There is a story of a man who dreamed that he died and found himself immediately in a large room. In the room was a huge banquet table filled with all sorts of delicious food. Around the banquet table were people seated on chairs, obviously hungry. But the chairs were five feet from the edge of the table and the people apparently could not get out of the chairs. Furthermore, their arms were not long enough to reach the food on the table.

In the dream there was one large spoon, five feet long. Everyone was fighting, quarreling, and pushing each other, trying to grab hold of that spoon. Finally, in an awful scene, one strong bully got hold of the spoon. He reached out, picked up some food, and turned it to feed himself, only to find that the spoon was so long he could not touch his mouth. The food fell off. Immediately, someone else grabbed the spoon and held it. The new owner reached to pick up the food, but again could not feed himself. The handle was too long.

In the dream, the man who was observing it all said to his guide, "This is hell—to have food and not be able to eat it." The guide replied, "Where do you think you are? This is hell. But this is not your place. Come with me."

And they went into another room. In this room there was also a long table filled with food, exactly as in the other room. Everyone was seated in chairs, and for some reason they too seemed unable to get out of their chairs.

Like the others, they were unable to reach the food on the table. Yet they had a satisfied, pleasant look on their faces. Only then did the visitor see the reason why. Exactly as before, there was only one spoon. It too had a handle five feet long. Yet no one was fighting for it. In fact, one man, who held the handle, reached out, picked up the food, and put it into the mouth of someone else, who ate it and was satisfied.

That person then took the spoon by the handle, reached for the food from the table, and put it to the mouth of the man who had just given him something to eat. And the guide said, "This is heaven."

There is a good message for soul mates in this allegory. You can create a little heaven on earth by helping each other get your needs met. By working in cooperation with one another, your own home can be a taste of heavenly blessings (see Eph. 1:3, 20; 2:6; 3:10).

In the great prayer that Jesus taught his disciples, he says: "Our Father in heaven, hallowed be your name, your kingdom come, your will be done on earth as it is in heaven" (Matt. 6:9–10). The implication is that our lives can enjoy a foretaste of heaven. Christ would not teach his followers a prayer that could not be fulfilled.

In the garden area behind our home, which is built on a steep slope, there is a large retaining wall. And on the top of this tall wall is a small statuary angel that sits at the corner and looks over us. It's a pretty sculpture, but it serves as more than a piece of art to us. Our retaining wall angel is a reminder that in our marriage we can have a little heaven right here on earth. And so can you.

FROM GOD'S WORD

Praise be to the God and Father of our Lord Jesus Christ, who has blessed us in the heavenly realms with every spiritual blessing in Christ. For he chose us in him before the creation of the world to be holy and blameless in his sight.

EPHESIANS 1:3–4

YOUR TURN

- Do you have any tangible reminders in your home that serve as an impetus for creating a little heaven on earth through your marriage?
- What selfish pattern do you see in yourself that you would like to change? How does it impact your marriage?
- How do you work cooperatively to meet each other's needs? Give some examples.
- What is a concrete step each of you can take right now to initiate a pattern of increased kindness in your marriage?
- Are there areas of your life where you are ruggedly independent or reluctant to accept help? Share with your partner how he or she can offer the type of assistance you desire.

SOUL TO SOUL

To deepen your spiritual intimacy this next week, make note of:

- What you gained from this session together.
- A pressure point in your partner's upcoming week you will pray about.
- A concrete kindness you can offer your partner this week.

PRAYER

Holy God, make us eager to give to one another. Help us to possess kindness toward each other in increasing measure. Enable us to work cooperatively to enjoy a foretaste of heaven in our home this very moment. This we pray with assurance. Amen.

Real-Life Soul Mates

A.J. and I had a strong and dazzling attraction to each other in the early days of our relationship. It wasn't just physical; on a soul level, we shared a passion for music, and for worship in particular. We knew that God had brought us together, and we dreamed about how he might one day use us in ministry.

Once the marriage license was signed, however, things went south fast. Remnants of childhood sexual abuse triggered a complete shutdown in the area of sexual intimacy before we had even really gotten started as a married couple. The wounds cut deep, fast.

As the protective walls went up, it became easy to separate emotionally, relationally, and spiritually too. The chaotic years of parenting three young children led to further disconnection, until we lived more like roommates than husband and wife.

At times the divide seemed so deep, so wide, that it was painful to even hope for things to change. Sometimes it can still feel that way. But we know that God is in our marriage, and we learn more every day about how pursuing him together is the bridge that can span the great divide.

When things aren't working in other areas of a relationship, it can be hard to risk vulnerability on a spiritual level. Yet spiritual intimacy acts as a port in the storms you're sure to face in your marriage. The key is in knowing that your port doesn't have to look like someone else's.

For us, the easiest way to connect to God is through worship. If you see us on a Sunday morning, we are abandoned to the music in sometimes embarrassing ways. And when A.J. plays worship music on the piano at home, peace pervades our space, and my heart is stilled and drawn back toward him. Toward "us."

I used to undervalue the spiritual discipline of worship because, frankly, it seems too easy. But it's how God wired us. And when it gets tempting to retreat to our separate corners—which happens more often than I'd like to admit—worship is how God leads us back to him and how he glues us together again.

Twenty-one years later, we can't claim to have arrived in the area of spiritual intimacy. But we're still together, and continually growing closer.

One day, one risk, and one song at a time.

A.J. and Constance Rhodes

A MILE IN MARRIAGE MOCCASINS

Rarely a month goes by that we do not receive a wedding invitation. And leading up to the month of June our mailbox seems to overflow. Because of our work with engaged couples, we attend a lot of weddings. And many of the weddings we attend include the traditional candle ceremony at some point in the service, usually near the end. The bride and groom each take a burning candle and light another candle, then blow out their own candles, symbolizing that the two have become one.

Every time we observe the lighting of a unity candle, however, we are reminded that marriage doesn't work like that. No one can blow out his or her personality, let alone that of his or her partner. Even after years of marriage, partners remain uniquely themselves. That's one of the big reasons why marriage is an ongoing challenge—and an adventure!

We hope you respect one another's individuality and uniqueness. Too many couples believe being married means being alike. And that causes problems. For it leads us to expect our spouse to be just like us, and when he or she isn't—which is most of the time—we become critical.

There is an old Sioux Indian prayer that gets at the solution to this common problem. It says, "O Great Spirit, grant me the wisdom to walk in another's moccasins before I criticize or pass judgment." Learning to walk in your mate's moccasins is at the heart of a healthy marriage relationship. Psychologists call it empathy, the rare capacity to put ourselves into the shoes of our partner and accurately see life from his or her perspective.

Empathy combines two important capacities: to analyze and to sympathize, to use our heads and to use our hearts. Our analytical capacities involve collecting facts and observing conditions. We look at a problem, we break it down into its causes, and we propose solutions. That's analyzing. Sympathizing is feeling for another person. It is feeling the pain of someone who is suffering or feeling the anger of a person in rage. Sympathizing and analyzing are the twin engines of empathy. One without the other is fine, but their true power is found in combination. We need to love with both our head and our heart to empathize.

The apostle Paul encouraged empathy in Hebrews when he said: "Continue to remember those in prison as if you were together with them in prison, and those who are mistreated as if you yourselves were suffering" (13:3). He also said, "We who are strong ought to bear with the failings of the weak and not to please ourselves" (Rom. 15:1).

When we empathize with our partner, we put aside our expectation that he or she should be like us. We accept the fact that our partner has brought a unique personality into our marriage and we ask ourselves questions like "What is *he* feeling? What pressures does *she* have to cope with? What does *he* fear? What does *she* need? How, if at all, should I help my spouse?"

The best model of empathy is our Lord himself. If Jesus Christ had been merely sympathetic to our plight, he would have watched our struggles from afar, shaking his head and feeling bad. If he had been merely analytical, he would have told us exactly what to do, stripping us of our freedom and solving all our problems for us. Instead, the Son of God chose to become one of us (see John 1:14; Luke 1:32; Phil. 2:7; Col. 1:15; 1 Tim. 2:5).

So before you jump to conclusions, before you criticize, before you pass judgment, use Jesus as your model and walk in your partner's shoes.

FROM GOD'S WORD

In your relationships with one another, have the same mindset as Christ Jesus: Who, being in very nature God, did not consider equality with God something to be used to his own advantage; rather, he made himself nothing by taking the very nature of a servant, being made in human likeness. And being found in appearance as a man, he humbled himself by becoming obedient to death—even death on a cross!

PHILIPPIANS 2:5–8

YOUR TURN

- While the word *empathy* is never used in the Bible, it is, in a sense, what the whole gospel message is about. Talk about the way empathy is ultimately demonstrated in the life of Christ.
- What is one area where you would especially like your spouse to empathize with you?
- It is easy to jump to conclusions and become critical without first understanding why your mate did something. What would allow you to catch yourself the next time you are tempted to do so?
- In what ways have you consciously or unconsciously

wished your partner was more like you? Are you ready to
let that expectation go?
- Give an example of a time you consciously tried to
  empathize with your partner. Was it hard work? What
  happened as a result of your effort?

SOUL TO SOUL

To deepen your spiritual intimacy this next week, make note of:

- What you gained from this session together.
- A pressure point in your partner's upcoming week you
  will pray about.
- A concrete kindness you can offer your partner this week.

PRAYER

*Christ Jesus, open the eyes of our hearts and the ears of our minds to grant
true empathy to our partner. Teach us to put ourselves in each other's shoes.
Help us to identify one another's feelings, pressures, fears, and needs. And
help us to do those things that make life better for each other. Amen.*

Real-Life Soul Mates

It became apparent early on in our marriage that though we're "one flesh," we approach our spiritual practices very differently, which made for challenges in our shared devotional life.

Morning person or night owl? Detail oriented or big idea? Practical or ideological? We are all of these! We learned to stop comparing ourselves and simply enjoy the common ground of worship we discovered in our great love of nature.

We established a Friday ritual of escaping to the woods along hiking trails or ski slopes of the Pacific Northwest. This is our Sabbath rest in God's cathedral. We pick out a trail based on time and energy constraints and head out early for our time of roaming. We remain quiet on the uphill, each in our own thoughts (perfect for the "night owl," who's still waking up). When we reach our destination, we enjoy our salami, cheese, apples, nuts, carrots, and hot tea and marvel at the glorious creation surrounding us. The thick evergreen forest, the bald eagles soaring in the blue sky above, the unique wildflowers, bumblebees, huckleberries, and chipmunks all offer a creation symphony, reminders of who God is, who we are, and the grand beauty and eternality of God's plans.

This leads to our time of reflection. What is God teaching us from the delicate ecosystem surrounding us? How do I sense God's Word in my life right now? Is it flooding my soul like spring rain, or is it sitting like snowpack, feeling a bit dormant but ready to nourish when called upon? Do I feel parched like a dusty trail in August, or am I courageous as I break trail after an overnight snowfall? Is God challenging us to something new, or is God calling us to continue to reach deeper into his sufficiency? What can we learn from this bee or that flower? Our time of reflection often leads to excellent conversations unencumbered by the distractions of civilization.

Our hikes provide needed space for bonding and restoration as a couple because, while we each hear from God differently in our separate activities all week, we encounter a common revelation in God's cathedral. We share and learn from each other's observations. Back home, we complete our Sabbath by preparing a delicious meal together, continuing the conversation by candlelight and on into the bedroom, celebrating all we've shared.

During our recent forty-day trek through the Alps, we spent day after day practicing this routine of *ritual, roaming, reflection,* and *restoration.* We never stop learning from each other or from the lessons of God's creation.

Richard and Donna Dahlstrom

Session Fifty-One

THE QUESTION THAT COULD CHANGE YOUR MARRIAGE

The oddsmakers say the chances are five in ten that a marriage will end in divorce. If one or both partners are still teenagers, they say the odds for divorce are even higher. If either partner witnessed an unhappy marriage at home, the odds increase again. If one or both partners come from broken homes, the odds rise yet higher. If either partner has been divorced, the odds soar. If there has been regular sexual involvement before marriage, or if either or both partners abuse alcohol or drugs, the odds skyrocket.

Well, regardless of your marriage "odds," we have a soul-searching question for you that will help you beat them. Are you ready? Ask yourself: *How would I like to be married to me?*

That simple question can do more to help you ensure the success of your marriage than just about anything else. Think about it. How would you rate you as a marriage partner? Are you easy to live with? How do you enrich the relationship? What are the positive qualities you bring to your marriage?

Learn the lesson Paul wrote about in 2 Corinthians: "We

do not dare to classify or compare ourselves with some who commend themselves. When they measure themselves by themselves and compare themselves with themselves, they are not wise" (10:12).

Every marriage is unique, and while there is no definitive list of qualities that describe good spouses, consider some of the traits that show up again and again in studies of lifelong love. Research, for example, has shown that partners who are easy to live with feel good about themselves. They are not unduly concerned over the impression they make on others. They can throw back their heads, breathe deep, and enjoy life. This kind of person is described in Galatians: "they can take pride in themselves alone, without comparing themselves to someone else" (6:4). People who make good lifelong marriage partners also have a way of passing over minor offenses and injustices. In other words, they are not easily offended (see Rom. 14:20; Prov. 17:9). Some spouses punish their partner with time in the penalty box for ordinary bruises which happen to people who play the game.

Partners who are easy to live with are cooperative. They get along. They understand what the psalmist meant in saying, "How good and pleasant it is [to] live together in unity" (133:1; see also Acts 4:32; Rom. 14:19). They also have an even and stable emotional tone. Nobody is attracted to an uncontrollable temper (see James 1:19–20). Good spouses communicate their needs openly and honestly (see Eph. 4:15). What they say is in sync with how they feel and what they want. They do not mask their feelings to protect their pride or even to avoid hurting their spouse's feelings. Instead, they share their innermost thoughts, the good and the bad (see Col. 3:12).

You may not have every advantage for a successful marriage; few do. But you can pray with the psalmist: "Search me, O God, and know my heart" (139:23). By searching your soul, by questioning your character, and by becoming easy to live with, you will exponentially increase the probability of making your marriage last a lifetime. Paul says that people who are easy to live with shine like stars in the universe (see Phil. 2:15).

FROM GOD'S WORD

For this very reason, make every effort to add to your faith goodness; and to goodness, knowledge; and to knowledge, self-control; and to self-control, perseverance; and to perseverance, godliness; and to godliness, mutual affection; and to mutual affection, love. For if you possess these qualities in increasing measure, they will keep you from being ineffective and unproductive in your knowledge of our Lord Jesus Christ.

2 PETER 1:5–8

YOUR TURN

- The Bible lists many admirable qualities, virtues, and traits. Out of the ones mentioned in the passage from 2 Peter, which ones do you find toughest to practice?
- Share with your partner how you think you might be difficult to live with at times. What qualities would make it hard for you to be married to you?
- Share with your partner the qualities he or she possesses that make it easy for you to be married to him or her.
- What makes it so difficult for most spouses to pass over minor offenses in marriage?
- Talk about one thing each of you is going to work on this week to become easier to live with.

SOUL TO SOUL

To deepen your spiritual intimacy this next week, make note of:

- What you gained from this session together.
- A pressure point in your partner's upcoming week you will pray about.
- A concrete kindness you can offer your partner this week.

PRAYER

Our God and Father, we long to know you more and serve you better. For it is only in relationship with you that our love for each other can truly grow. Help us to keep in mind who we are in this partnership. Show us the way to become better marriage partners. Help us to work on those qualities that bring glory to you and joy to each other. Strengthen us by your Spirit for every good work. Amen.

Real-Life Soul Mates

Alyssa and I prize our Sabbath. After just a few years of marriage, we've learned that to be truly Christ-centered in our marriage, we need to rest together. Our relationship is best when we are "sabbathing." And by that I don't mean vegging out watching television or doing errands.

I think a true Sabbath is woven into the fabric of creation. Each week, humans are designed to cease "doing"—to be a human being, not a human doing.

Our Sabbath includes a good and relaxing meal together. And it involves playing. That often means hanging out at the beach near our home, walking hand-in-hand, sometimes swimming. Always talking and praying.

We've built Sabbath into the rhythm of our marriage. Our Sabbath has become an anchor point that we count on. We look forward to it. If the week was crazy, it's where we catch up. If the week was tiring, it's where we rest. If the week was hard, it's where we find healing and restoration in our spirits together.

Abraham Heschel, a Jewish thinker, says that if the temple is sacred space, then the Sabbath is sacred time. And he's exactly right. Our dedicated time together each week has become sacred to us. We protect it. We don't treat it lightly. We say no to whatever interferes with it. After all, we are image bearers of Christ. And our Sabbath is a "yes" to our future as a married couple. It's looking into the future and saying "on earth as it is in heaven."

A cousin of the Sabbath for us is hospitality. For us, so many of the important things in life seem to happen around our table. It's where stories are told. It's where relationships are formed. It's where learning takes place. And as a couple, a team, we get to create those little pockets of God's presence at the table for our guests by how we host, love, and serve each other.

So the big question I'd ask the two of you is: Are you making a priority of resting and playing together? Are you celebrating the gift of the table?

We all find our own pathway as couples for walking with God together, but for us, we join our spirits in these two ways—Sabbath and hospitality—and we'd encourage you to consider them, too.

Jeff and Alyssa Bethke

Session Fifty-Two

SOUL TO SOUL
FOREVER AND EVER

Last summer our family gathered around a large circular table in an elegant restaurant that has unofficially become the backdrop for many of our most meaningful family celebrations. For decades, literally, our family has gathered here from around the country to mark holidays, birthdays, graduations, promotions, and farewells. But this time was different. The dinner was a celebration of Mom and Dad's fiftieth wedding anniversary. They didn't want a big party. This celebration was strictly a family affair.

The food, as always, was exquisite. The anniversary cake was lovely. The presents were nice, but not worthy of such a noble occasion. What impressed us most about the entire event, however, wasn't tangible. It was something my father said. We had just offered grace and thanked God for the family and the many years Mom and Dad had lived together. Then, before picking up his fork, he looked around the table and said: "I can't believe it has been fifty years! The time is so short!"

The rest of the meal was devoted to reminiscing. Mom talked about the times when each of her three sons was born. She could describe in detail the various homes we lived in. Dad talked about the churches and colleges he and Mom had served. There was the first pastorate they took during the Korean War and the transition to being a college president during the Mideast oil crisis. They both reminisced about their first trip to London and many other journeys around the globe. They must certainly have had some hard times, like all married couples do, but all they seemed to remember were things they enjoyed together.

Fifty years! What will your marriage look like in fifty years? What will you reminisce about? Can you imagine your future together? "There is surely a future hope for you, and your hope will not be cut off" (Prov. 23:18).

"By wisdom a house is built," says Proverbs, "and through understanding it is established; through knowledge its rooms are filled with rare and beautiful treasures" (24:3–4). After fifty years, what memorable treasures will your house of love include?

Something else struck us about Mom and Dad's fiftieth wedding anniversary—their utter dependence on God. It is impossible to separate their spiritual formation from their marital maturity. They are living proof to us that no single factor does more to cultivate oneness and a meaningful sense of purpose in marriage than a shared commitment to spiritual discovery.

Sharing life's ultimate meaning with another person is the call of soul mates. Spirituality is to your marriage as yeast is to a loaf of bread. We have said to hundreds of couples: Ultimately, your spiritual commitment will determine whether your marriage rises successfully or falls disappointingly flat.

Will you look back while celebrating fifty years of marriage and say, "I can't believe time is so short"? We pray you will. For, "As a bridegroom rejoices over his bride, so will your God rejoice over you" (Isa. 62:5).

FROM GOD'S WORD

I will betroth you to me forever; I will betroth you in righteousness and justice, in love and compassion. I will betroth you in faithfulness, and you will acknowledge the Lord.

HOSEA 2:19–20

YOUR TURN

- Can you sense that God is rejoicing over you and your marriage? How do you, as a couple, join in his celebration of you?
- How is your marital maturity tied to your spiritual development? Can you separate the two? Why or why not?
- Talk about the meaning of your wedding anniversary. How do you like to mark this important milestone?
- What are the signs in your relationship right now that indicate you and your partner are on your way to becoming lifelong soul mates?
- In your mind's eye, what will your fiftieth wedding anniversary look like? What emotions will you be experiencing? What will you be most thankful for?

SOUL TO SOUL

To deepen your spiritual intimacy this next week, make note of:

- What you gained from this session together.
- A pressure point in your partner's upcoming week you will pray about.
- A concrete kindness you can offer your partner this week.

PRAYER

God of peace, sanctify us through and through. Fill our whole spirit, soul, and body with a rich love, and keep our marriage securely planted in the person of Christ. It is in your faithful hands we entrust our marriage and ask for a lifetime of happiness and mutual helpfulness. Amen.

Real-Life Soul Mates

My romance with Lisa started off with me kidding her about her (in my opinion) quirky quiet times. Having been a morning person all my life, I thought quiet times were best done in the morning, but Lisa is decidedly *not* a morning person, so in college she'd wake up just in time to make it to her first class, come back to the dorms around lunchtime, and then go up onto the roof to sit in the sun with her Bible and pray.

"You've got to be kidding me!" I said. "Who goes up onto the roof at noon and calls that a legitimate quiet time?"

Lisa couldn't respond at the moment, but two weeks later she knocked on my dorm room door. When I opened it, she smiled, opened up my Bible, and showed me Acts 10:9: "About noon the following day . . . Peter went up on the roof to pray."

Score one for Lisa.

As a dating couple, we read through books of the Bible together and frequently prayed together, but when kids came along and I started commuting to work, my early morning lifestyle and her nighttime efficiency made concerted spiritual devotions together difficult. But both of us are deeply fed and ministered to by our individual devotions. We may not pray and study the Bible at the same time, but we study the words of and pray to the same God, and that joint practice has immeasurably blessed our marriage.

The reality is that we are simply a more loving, intimate couple when we both take devotion to God seriously. First John 4:19 says, "We love because he first loved us." When we allow God's love and truth to shape us—regardless of what time of day it is—we act as more loving spouses.

Ministering together is a major part of our mutual devotion, and that has fueled our love as much as anything. When I see how the Holy Spirit uses Lisa, and Lisa sees how God uses me, our respect for each other grows. Letting God use you is a cheap but efficient way of building mutual esteem—but it works, and it's powerful, and it's wonderful to be brother and sister in Christ as well as husband and wife.

I wish Lisa and I were better at worshiping together on a daily basis, but I'm grateful that both of us find our souls filled and our love renewed by daily devotion to God—even if those devotions don't take place at the same time.

Gary and Lisa Thomas

BIOGRAPHIES OF REAL-LIFE SOUL MATES

Dan and Rebecca Allender grew up in the same hometown and began dating in college. Dan serves as professor of counseling at the Seattle School of Theology and Psychology and is the author of *The Wounded Heart* and *The Healing Path*. Dan and Rebecca and their three children Annie, Amanda, and Andrew live on Bainbridge Island, Washington.

Leith and Charleen Anderson have known each other all of their lives. They grew up in New Jersey but have lived much of their lives in Edina, Minnesota, where Leith served as pastor of Wooddale Church. He currently serves as the president of the National Association of Evangelicals.

Jeff and Alyssa Bethke are both authors who are currently living in Maui, Hawaii. They also make YouTube videos (which have been seen collectively well over sixty million times), and they host a podcast that can be found on iTunes. They have a little girl named Kinsley and a family dog named Aslan. Learn more at jeffbethke .com or alyssajoy.me.

Pat and Shirley Boone have been married over sixty years. Though Pat is a movie actor, television host, and successful recording artist, and though Shirley is a successful author in her own right, they are both most proud of their four married daughters and fifteen grandchildren.

Stuart and Jill Briscoe have been married for more than fifty-five years. They have three children (David, Judy, and Peter) and thirteen grandchildren. Stuart is the former senior pastor at Elmbrook Church in Brookfield, Wisconsin. They have authored over sixty books.

Dale and Nina Bronner married in 1984 and are parents of four daughters and one son. Bishop Dale Bronner is founder and senior pastor of Word of Faith Family Worship Cathedral in Atlanta, Georgia, and author of several books, including *Pass the Baton*. Learn more at woffamily.org.

Brice and Shelene Bryan have been married for twenty-five years and have two children. Shelene is the founder of Skip1.org. She is author of *Love, Skip, Jump* and *Ridiculous Faith*. Brice is an attorney practicing law in Southern California.

Jim and Cathy Burns have been married nearly forty years. Jim is the president of HomeWord and executive director of the HomeWord Center for Youth and Family at Azusa Pacific University. Cathy is a busy stay-at-home mom and manages to teach Sunday school and women's Bible studies. They make their home in Southern California and have three daughters: Christy, Rebecca, and Heidi.

Francis and Lisa Chan started Cornerstone Community Church in Simi Valley, California, the same year they married. Francis is the author of *Crazy Love*, and they are both authors of *You and Me Forever*. They have seven children.

Gary and Karolyn Chapman have been married for more than forty-five years. Gary is author of *The Five Love Languages* and *The Marriage You've Always Wanted*. Learn more at 5lovelanguages.com. Also visit startmarriageright.com.

Chap and Dee Clark have been married more than thirty-five years and have three adult children. Chap, whose books include

Sticky Faith, is professor and chair of the Youth, Family, and Culture Department in the School of Theology at Fuller Theological Seminary. Dee is a marriage and family therapist.

John Mark and Tammy Comer have three children: Jude, Moses, and Sunday. John Mark is pastor of Bridgetown: A Jesus Church, which is part of a family of churches in Portland, Oregon. Learn more at johnmarkcomer.com.

Winston and Rachel Cruze married on December 19, 2009, and recently had a baby girl, Amelia. Rachel is coauthor with her father, Dave Ramsey, of *Smart Money, Smart Kids*. Learn more at RachelCruze.com.

Ted and Amy Cunningham founded Woodland Hills Family Church in Branson, Missouri, in 2002. They met at Liberty University in 1995 and married the next year. They live in Branson with their two children, Corynn and Carson. Ted and Amy are the authors of *Come to the Family Table* and *The Power of Home 90-Day Devotional*. Learn more at www.woodhills.org.

Richard and Donna Dahlstrom married in 1979 and have three adult children, all thriving outdoor enthusiasts. Richard has served as senior pastor at Bethany Community Church in Seattle, Washington, since 1995. He also shares his gift of teaching with Torchbearers Missionary Fellowship at Bible schools and conference centers around the world. His books include *O2: Breathing New Life into Faith* and *Colors of Hope*. Learn more at www.stepbystep-journey.com.

Jim and Jean Daly married in 1986 and have two sons. Jim is host of Focus on the Family's daily radio broadcast. His books include *ReFocus* and *The Good Dad*. Learn more at focusonthefamily.com.

Justin and Trisha Davis are bloggers, authors, speakers, and founders of RefineUs Ministries. By sharing their story of pain, loss, and redemption, RefineUs is igniting a movement to build healthy marriages. They are the coauthors of *Beyond Ordinary: When a Good Marriage Just Isn't Good Enough.*

Jeff and Shaunti Feldhahn are bestselling authors, popular speakers, and groundbreaking social researchers. But they started as an average semiconfused couple (he's an attorney, she was a Wall Street analyst) who just didn't understand each other, and have since used their analytical backgrounds to help other couples learn the little things that make a big difference in relationships. Jeff and Shaunti have authored *For Women Only* and *For Men Only*. The Feldhahns married in 1994, have two teenage children, and live in Atlanta, Georgia. Learn more at www.shaunti.com.

Jim and Rosemary Garlow married in 2014. They have eight children and nine grandchildren. Jim is pastor of Skyline Church in La Mesa, California, and he has written eleven books, including the *New York Times* bestseller *Cracking Da Vinci's Code*.

Craig and Jeanette Gross have been married for sixteen years. Craig is the founder of XXX Church, a ministry dedicated to helping people all over the world with sexual struggles and temptations. He is also author of over twelve books. Craig and Jeanette live in Los Angeles with their two children, Nolan and Elise. Learn more at craiggross.com.

Gary and Jorie Gulbranson married in 1973. Gary is senior pastor of Westminster Chapel in Bellevue, Washington. Jorie has been a junior high school teacher. Both Gary and Jorie have published articles on various counseling issues. They enjoy golf, exploring new cities, and listening to and playing the saxophone and violin.

Jack and Anna Hayford met in college in 1952 and have been married more than sixty years. Jack is the founding pastor of The Church On the Way in Van Nuys, California. He has written numerous books and songs, including the widely sung "Majesty." Anna is a supportive partner who keeps her joy and sense of humor in the midst of a continually mushrooming ministry.

Bill and Liz Curtis Higgs married March 14, 1986, have two grown children, and two tabby cats that make Bill crazy (and make Liz happy). Liz is the author of more than thirty books, including her bestseller, *Bad Girls of the Bible*, and she has spoken for more than 1,700 conferences around the world. Bill Higgs, PhD, serves as director of operations for Liz's speaking and writing office, and is the author of the novel *Eden Hill*. Find Liz online at www.LizCurtisHiggs.com.

Chris and Tammy Hodges were married on May 24, 1986, and have been in full-time ministry their whole married life. They currently serve as founding and senior pastors of Church of the Highlands in Birmingham, Alabama. They have five children. Chris has authored two books, *Fresh Air* and *Four Cups*. Learn more at churchofthehighlands.com.

Michael and Gail Hyatt have been married for thirty-seven years and have five daughters, five grandsons, and three granddaughters. Michael is the author of *Platform: Get Noticed in a Noisy World* and is the founder of Platform University. Learn more at MichaelHyatt.com.

Kevin and Sande Leman have been married for over four decades and have five children and two grandchildren. Kevin is the *New York Times* bestselling author of numerous titles, including *Have a New Kid by Friday*, *Sheet Music*, *Sex Begins in the Kitchen*, and *The Birth Order Book*. He's appeared numerous times on *Fox & Friends*, *Oprah*, *The View*, *Today*, *Good Morning America*, and *700 Club*.

Jeff and Brandy Little have been married for twenty years and have four children—two teenagers, a ten-year-old, and a four-year-old. In 2002 they planted Milestone Church in Keller, Texas, with just a handful of people. Today the church serves thousands throughout the Dallas/Fort Worth region.

Walt and Meg Meeker have been married for thirty-five years and have two adult children. Walt is an internist and pediatrician and Meg is a pediatrician. They practice in Traverse City, Michigan, and enjoy medical mission trips to South America. Meg is also author of *Strong Fathers, Strong Daughters*, and she is a spokesperson for Food for the Hungry.

Mike and Carmen Meeks are leading EastLake Church in Chula Vista, California, a congregation with seven campuses. They have two amazing adult children, the best daughter-in-law and son-in-law anyone could hope for, and seven exceptional grandchildren.

Michael Jr. and Ebony were married in 2004 and have five children. Ebony has written a pre-marriage book for women called *Before He Finds You*. As a stand-up comedian, Michael Jr.'s television appearances include *The Tonight Show*, *Oprah*, *Jimmy Kimmel Live*, and *Comedy Central*. He was also in the Sony Pictures movie *War Room*, which hit number one at the box office. If you want to see Michael Jr. live or see some hilarious video go to michaeljr.com for more information.

Mark and Heidi Mittelberg live in the suburbs of Chicago with their daughter, Emma Jean, and son, Matthew. An author, speaker, and evangelism strategist, Mark served as the evangelism leader for the Willow Creek Association and coauthored the book and the training course *Becoming a Contagious Christian*. Heidi has a background in teaching, which she uses to help direct a private Christian school. She also serves as a vocalist at Willow Creek Community Church.

Keith and Beth Moore have been married since 1978 and have two grown daughters, Amanda and Melissa. Beth is a speaker, teacher, and writer of bestselling books and Bible studies. They live in Houston, Texas, where Beth is president and founder of Living Proof Ministries.

Jim and Sue Nicodem have been married for more than thirty years and have three adult children. Since 1984, Jim has been senior pastor of Christ Community Church near Chicago. He's the author of *Prayer Coach* and the four-book Bible Savvy series.

John and Nancy Ortberg have been married more than thirty years and they have three grown children. Nancy is a sought-after speaker and author. Her bestselling books include *Seeing in the*

Dark. John is the senior pastor at Menlo Park Presbyterian Church in Menlo Park, California, and his bestselling books include *The Life You've Always Wanted*.

Dave and Sharon Ramsey have been married for more than thirty years and have three adult children: Denise, Rachel, and Daniel. Dave is America's trusted voice on money and business. He's authored five *New York Times* bestselling books. *The Dave Ramsey Show* is heard by more than 8.5 million listeners each week on more than 550 radio stations. Learn more at daveramsey.com.

A.J. and Constance Rhodes have been married since 1994. They live in Franklin, Tennessee, with their three children and an overly excitable Chihuahua named Mercy. A.J. works at Capitol Christian Music Group. Constance is an author and the founder and CEO of FINDINGbalance, a nonprofit helping people find balance with food, weight, and wellness. Learn more at findingbalance.com.

Denny and Marilyn Rydberg grew up in the Pacific Northwest but now live in Colorado Springs, where Denny is in his twenty-third year serving as the president of Young Life. Prior to that, Marilyn and Denny served nine years as the directors of University Ministries at University Presbyterian Church in Seattle. They have four adult children and five grandchildren.

Mark and Kate Schultz married in 2005. Kate is a physician and Mark is an award-winning Christian singer/songwriter. In 2011, Mark and Kate started Remember Me Mission, a nonprofit dedicated to helping orphans all over the world. Proceeds from Schultz's music and other creative projects go toward health care and education for orphans at home and abroad. Learn more at markschultzmusic.com.

Ronald and Arbutus Sider have been married for more than forty-five years and are the parents of three children. Arbutus is a family therapist, and Ron is founder of Evangelicals for Social Action, a think tank which seeks to develop biblical solutions to social and economic problems.

Donna and Ed Stetzer have been married almost thirty years. Donna is a stay-at-home mom and Ed is executive director of LifeWay Research. Learn more at edstetzer.com.

Dave and Beth Stone were married on November 1, 1985. Dave is senior pastor of Southeast Christian Church in Louisville, Kentucky. Among Dave's books are the Faithful Families series on parenting. Learn more at www.southeastchristian.org.

Ken and Joni Eareckson Tada have been married for over thirty years. Ken is retired from thirty-two years of teaching and now serves as director of ministry development for Joni and Friends, an organization that accelerates Christian outreach in the disability community. Ken is an avid fly fisherman and helps to lead Wild Adventures, a fishing ministry for men. Joni is founder and CEO of Joni and Friends. Joni is the author of numerous bestselling books, including *When God Weeps*, *Diamonds in the Dust*, and *A Step Further*. Learn more at joniandfriends.org.

Art and Lysa TerKeurst live in North Carolina and have five children. Art is the owner/operator of a Chick-fil-A and is passionate about leadership. Lysa is a *New York Times* bestselling author and president of Proverbs 31 Ministries.

Gary and Lisa Thomas have been married for thirty-one years and have three grown children. Gary is a regular blogger on marital issues (www.garythomas.com/blog) and is the author of *Sacred Marriage*, *A Lifelong Love*, and many other books that together have sold over a million copies worldwide. Learn more at www.garythomas.com.

John and Barbi Townsend have been married more than thirty years and are the parents of two children. John is a psychologist and author in Newport Beach, California. Barbi is a former elementary school teacher and administrator.

Casey and Wendy Treat founded Christian Faith Center in Seattle, Washington, with thirty people. Today the church has three campuses and more than ten thousand people attending weekly.

The Treats also host *Your Unlimited Life,* a weekly television program that broadcasts nationally and internationally.

John and Cindy Trent have been married for thirty years, have two daughters, and live in Phoenix, Arizona. John, a nationally known author and speaker, is the president of the Center for Strong Families, and Cindy is a retired elementary school teacher.

Keith and Fawn Weaver have been married for twelve years and live in Los Angeles. Fawn is the *USA Today* and *New York Times* bestselling author of *The Argument-Free Marriage* and *Happy Wives Club.* She is the founder of the Happy Wives Club, a community of close to one million women in 110 countries around the world.

Mike and Kandice Weaver married in 2005, live in Nashville, and have three children: Eli, Zeke, and Naomi. Mike is the lead singer for Big Daddy Weave, an award-winning contemporary Christian band. Visit BigDaddyWeave.com.

Dave and Ashley Willis are the founders of StrongerMarriages .com and the authors of *iVow: Secrets to a Stronger Marriage* and *Marriage Minute.* They have four young sons and live near Augusta, Georgia, where Dave serves as a teaching pastor for Stevens Creek Church.

Pete and Brandi Wilson planted Cross Point Church in Nashville, Tennessee, in 2002. Their ministry has grown to seven locations throughout Middle Tennessee. Pete is the bestselling author of *Plan B* along with *Empty Promises, Let Hope In,* and *What Keeps You Up at Night.* Brandi co-leads a ministry called Leading and Loving It, which focuses on pastors' wives and women in ministry. She has also authored a book by the same title. They have three sons: Jett, Gage, and Brewer.

Zig and Jean Ziglar were married for sixty-five years before Zig passed away in 2012. They met in Jackson, Mississippi, when he was seventeen and she was sixteen. Zig was a bestselling author, salesman, and motivational speaker. Jean worked closely with Zig in the writing of his books and his daily newspaper column.

GIVE THE VERY BEST TO

You won't find a more personalized and powerful pre-marriage assessment than SYMBIS.

"The SYMBIS Assessment rocks! We learned so much about our relationship and feel incredibly confident about our future together."
-Toni & Chris

YOUR RELATIONSHIP

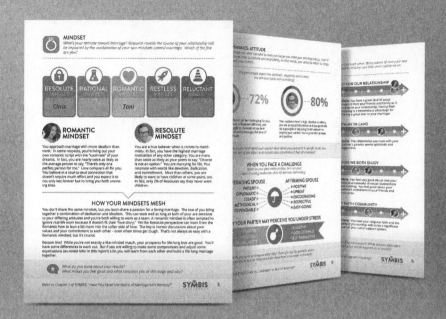

EVERYTHING YOU NEED TO KNOW ABOUT:

- **Your Personalities** – *discover your strengths*
- **Your Love Life** – *cultivate deeper passion*
- **Your Fight Types** – *discover your "hot topics"*
- **Your Talk Styles** – *crack your intimacy codes*
- **Your Money Methods** – *kick financial woes to the curb*

And so much more. **Plus**, *it works seamlessly with the SYMBIS book and his/her workbooks.*

Take the assessment: SYMBISassessment.com

YOUR ONE-STOP SHOP FOR
PRE-MARRIAGE

We've got everything you need to launch lifelong love.

LesandLeslie.com

book

OVER ONE MILLION COPIES SOLD

SAVING YOUR
MARRIAGE
BEFORE IT STARTS

Seven Questions to Ask Before - and After - You Marry

SYMBIS

Drs. Les & Leslie Parrott
#1 New York Times Best Selling Authors

NEWLY EXPANDED EDITION

SYMBIS
SAVING YOUR MARRIAGE BEFORE IT STARTS
ASSESSMENT

Report for:

TONI DAY & CHRIS CRARY
Date Completed: 9/12/2014

Prepared by:
DRS. LES AND LESLIE PARROTT
info@lesandleslie.com
206.123.4321

SYMBISAssessment.com

MARRIAGE
MENTORING
.COM

training

OVER ONE MILLION COPIES SOLD

SAVING YOUR
SECOND
MARRIAGE
BEFORE IT STARTS

Nine Questions to Ask Before - and After - You Remarry

SYMBIS

Drs. Les & Leslie Parrott
#1 New York Times Bestselling Authors

NEWLY EXPANDED EDITION

assessment

remarriage book

DVD

his & hers
workbooks

WORKBOOK FOR MEN

SAVING YOUR
MARRIAGE
BEFORE IT STARTS
Seven Questions to Ask Before - and After - You Marry

SYMBIS

Drs. Les & Leslie Parrott

WORKBOOK FOR WOMEN

SAVING YOUR
MARRIAGE
BEFORE IT STARTS
Seven Questions to Ask Before - and After - You Marry

SYMBIS

Drs. Les & Leslie Parrott

SAVING YOUR
MARRIAGE
BEFORE IT STARTS
Seven Questions to Ask
Before - and After - You Marry   SEVEN SESSIONS

Drs. Les & Leslie Parrott

ZONDERVAN   DVD

Bible
studies

WORKBOOK FOR MEN

SAVING YOUR
SECOND
MARRIAGE
BEFORE IT STARTS
Nine Questions to Ask Before - and After - You Remarry

SYMBIS

Drs. Les & Leslie Parrott

WORKBOOK FOR WOMEN

SAVING YOUR
SECOND
MARRIAGE
BEFORE IT STARTS
Nine Questions to Ask Before - and After - You Remarry

SYMBIS

Drs. Les & Leslie Parrott

SAVING YOUR
SECOND
MARRIAGE
BEFORE IT STARTS
Nine Questions to Ask
And - and After - You Remarry   NINE SESSIONS

Drs. Les & Leslie Parrott

ZONDERVAN   DVD

remarriage
DVD

remarriage
workbooks